Questioning in the Secondary School

Teachers ask thousands of questions in a year. The ability to ask intelligent and searching questions, to use questioning for different purposes and to know what to do with the answer is crucial to teachers of all subjects. It is one of the core teaching skills that informs good practice and can help improve pupils' learning.

In *Questioning in the Secondary School*, Ted Wragg and George Brown explore:

- the range of questions that teachers can ask, from those requiring simple recall of information right up to those that stimulate complex reasoning, imagination and speculation
- the various strategies open to teachers that, through a combination of activities and discussion points, help them to build up a repertoire of ideas, approaches and techniques which are suitable for various situations
- the ways in which teachers can evaluate the effectiveness of their questions in the classroom

Children's own thinking and learning can be improved significantly if they have the opportunity to respond to teachers' questions and to enjoy the process of interaction with them. This book concentrates on everyday use of questions in the classroom, whether in organised groups, for individual learning or for whole class activities.

Ted Wragg is Professor of Education at Exeter University and the author of over 40 books. He has directed numerous research projects, analysed hundreds of lessons and writes a regular column for the *Times Educational Supplement*.

George Brown is a Professor in Education at Nottingham University and is also an Education Consultant.

Successful Teaching Series

This set of practical resource books for teachers focuses on the classroom. The first editions were best sellers and these new editions will be equally welcomed by teachers eager to improve their teaching skills. Each book contains:

- practical, written and oral activities for individual and group use at all stages of professional development
- transcripts of classroom conversation and teacher feedback and photographs of classroom practice to stimulate discussion
- succinct and practical explanatory text

Titles in the *Successful Teaching Series* are

Class Management in the Primary School
E. C. Wragg

Class Management in the Secondary School
E. C. Wragg

Assessment and Learning in the Primary School
E. C. Wragg

Assessment and Learning in the Secondary School
E. C. Wragg

Explaining in the Primary School
E. C. Wragg and G. Brown

Explaining in the Secondary School
E. C. Wragg and G. Brown

Questioning in the Primary School
E. C. Wragg and G. Brown

Questioning in the Secondary School
E. C. Wragg and G. Brown

The first editions were published in the *Leverhulme Primary Project Classroom Skills Series*.

Questioning in the Secondary School

E. C. Wragg and G. Brown

London and New York

First published as *Questioning* in 1993
by Routledge
This new revised edition first published 2001
by RoutledgeFalmer
11 New Fetter Lane, London EC4P 4EE

Simultaneously published in the USA and Canada
by RoutledgeFalmer
29 West 35th Street, New York, NY 10001

RoutledgeFalmer is an imprint of the Taylor & Francis Group

© 2001 E. C. Wragg and G. Brown

Typeset in Palatino by Bookcraft Ltd, Stroud, Gloucestershire
Printed and bound in Great Britain by Bell & Bain Ltd, Glasgow

British Library Cataloguing in Publication Data
A catalogue record for this book is available from the British Library

Library of Congress Cataloging in Publication Data
Wragg, E. C. (Edward Conrad)
    Questioning in the secondary school / E. C. Wragg and
    G. Brown.
        p. cm. – (Successful teaching series)
    Includes bibliographical references.
      1. Questioning. 2 Education, Secondary. I. Brown, George, 1935–
    II. Title. III. Successful teaching series (London, England)

    LB1027.44. W73 2001
    373.13'7–dc21   00–051800

ISBN 0–415–24952–X

Contents

Preface

Improving the quality of learning in secondary schools, and preparing children for what will probably be a long and complex life in the twenty-first century, requires the highest quality of teaching and professional training. The *Successful Teaching Series* focuses on the essence of classroom competence, on those professional skills which make a real difference to children, like the ability to explain clearly, to ask intelligent and thought-provoking questions, to manage classes effectively and to use the assessment of progress to enhance pupils' learning.

'Success' may be defined in many ways. For some it is seen purely in test scores, for others it is a broader issue, involving the whole child. In this series we often report what has been done by teachers judged to be successful, or unsuccessful, on several criteria: head teachers' assessments, pupil progress measures, esteem from fellow teachers or from children. Skilful teachers ensure that their classes learn something worthwhile, unskilful ones may turn off that delicate trip switch in children's psyche which keeps their minds open to life-long learning.

Experienced teachers have engaged in hundreds of exchanges every single day of their career, thousands in a year, millions over a professional lifetime. Teaching consists of dozens of favoured strategies that become embedded in deep structures, for there is no time for people to re-think every single move in a busy classroom. Many decisions are made by teachers in less than a second, so once these *deep structures* have been laid down, they are not always amenable to change, even if a school has a well-developed professional development programme. Reflecting on practice alone or with colleagues enables teachers to think about what they do away from the immediate pressures of rapid interaction and speedy change.

Rejecting the notion that there is only one way to teach, this series of books explores some of the many strategies available to teachers, as well as the patterns of classroom organisation which best assist pupil learning. It demonstrates throughout that teachers, even when working to predetermined work schemes and curricula, must forge their own ways of teaching in the light of the context in which they operate and the evidence available to them from different sources. The series is rooted in classroom observation research over several decades and is designed to assist teachers at all stages of their professional development.

The series also contains an element that is unusual in most of the books aimed at helping teachers. Some of the activities assume that teaching should not just be something that teachers do *to* their pupils, but rather *with* them, so they involve teachers and their classes working together to improve teaching and learning, pupils acting as partners, not merely as passive recipients of professional wizardry. Thus the books on class management consider such matters as self-discipline; those on questioning and explaining look at pupils interacting with each other; the ones on assessment address how children can learn from being assessed and also how they can appraise their own work. When children become adults they will have to be able to act autonomously during much of their lives, so learning early to take more and more responsibility for their own progress is crucial.

The books will be useful for:

- practising teachers,
- student teachers,
- college and university tutors, local and national inspectors and advisers,
- school-based in-service co-ordinators, advisory teachers,
- school mentors, appraisers and head teachers.

Like others in the series, this book can be used as part of initial or in-service programmes in school. The text can also be read by individuals as a source of ideas and will be helpful in teacher appraisal, developing professional awareness both for those being appraised and for their appraisers. The suggested activities have been tried out extensively by experienced teachers and those in pre-service training and revised in the light of their comments. The series will provoke discussion, help teachers reflect on their current and future practice and encourage them to look behind, and ask questions about, everyday classroom events.

Acknowledgements

Our thanks to the many members of our research teams, especially Gill Haynes, Caroline Wragg, Rosemary Chamberlin, Felicity Wikeley, Kay Wood, Sarah Crowhurst, Clive Carré, Trevor Kerry, Pauline Dooley, Allyson Trotter, Barbara Janssen, Sheila Armstrong and Rowena Edmondson, who between them have observed over two thousand lessons and interviewed teachers, pupils, parents and classroom assistants in hundreds of primary and secondary schools.

We should also like to express our gratitude to the many teachers who teach successfully on a daily basis. A number of the teachers shown at work in the books in the *Successful Teaching Series* are recipients of Platos, which are given to the national winners at the annual Teaching Awards ceremony.

The photographs in this book were taken by Fred Jarvis and Ted Wragg. The cartoons are by Jonathan Hall.

Aims and content

Imagine asking one of your neighbours, 'How many legs has an insect got?' or, 'What is three-quarters, expressed as a decimal?' In normal life you would probably be locked away if you went up to people and asked them large numbers of questions, the answers to which you already knew. It would be regarded as a somewhat rude invasion of their privacy, a breach of their personal space, or even as an extremely weird form of behaviour. Yet regular interrogation is part of the normal repertoire of teachers' classroom skills. Every day teachers ask dozens, even hundreds of questions, thousands in a single year, over a million during a professional lifetime. Intelligent questioning is a valuable part of interactive teaching. Inept handling of questions, however, leads to confusion and misunderstanding. Questions are often a central part of explanations – which we describe more fully in *Explaining in the Secondary School* in this series – and so lie at the very heart of successful teaching.

This book has been written to help young and experienced teachers in service in secondary schools to:

(a) reflect upon their uses of questions;
(b) develop their approaches to preparing, using and evaluating their own questions;
(c) explore ways in which pupils may be encouraged to question and to provide answers.

Children's own thinking and learning can be improved significantly if they have the opportunity to respond to teachers' questions and to enjoy the process of interaction with them. The principal focus of this book, therefore, is on everyday questions and questioning within the classroom, whether that classroom is organised in groups, for individual learning, or for whole class activities.

The contents are partly based on studies of questioning we have carried out during research projects in primary and secondary schools. We have analysed several thousand questions and their outcomes, by watching lessons, as well as by studying audio and videotapes and transcripts of the lessons. We have subsequently analysed them in the light of the discussions with the teachers and pupils involved in them.

The book is organised into the following six units. As befits a text on questioning, each unit addresses a key question. Within each unit are summaries of relevant research, activities and tasks to try out on one's own or with colleagues or pupils. There are also various guidelines and suggestions on questioning.

Unit 1 begins with the fundamental question: Why do we ask questions? It then considers the related questions: why do teachers ask questions, and why do pupils ask questions?

Unit 2 is concerned with what kind of questions are asked in the classroom and how they might usefully be classified.

Unit 3 focuses on the tactics of questioning, exploring such matters as the sequencing of questions, for questions often occur in chains.

Unit 4 deals with types of lesson, showing how different questions may be needed for different kinds of activity.

Unit 5 suggests ways of exploring how pupils learn and also ways in which they might become involved in thinking about their own questions.

Unit 6 provides a framework for exploring approaches to preparing key questions that might be included in lessons, and in some cases might even form the central part of the lessons.

HOW TO USE THIS BOOK

The six units constitute substantial course material for the topic 'questioning'. The activities and text are suitable for in-service and professional studies courses as well as for individual use.

The text may be read as a book in its own right; all the *activities* can be undertaken either by individual teachers or by members of a group working together on the topic.

The discussion activities can be used in group meetings, for example, or as part of staff discussion during a school's INSET day. The individual reader can use these as a prompt for reflection and planning.

The written activities are intended to be worked on individually but also lend themselves to group discussion when completed.

The practical activities are designed to be done in the teacher's own classroom or by student teachers on teaching practice or when they are teaching children brought into the training institution for professional work.

The book can either be used alone or in conjunction with other books in the *Successful Teaching Series*. Those responsible for courses, therefore, may well wish to put together exercises and activities from several of the books in this series to make up their own course as part of a general professional skills development programme, either in initial training or of whole school professional development. Usually the discussion and written activities described will occupy between an hour and ninety minutes and classroom activities completed in about an hour, though this may vary, depending on the context.

Many of the issues covered in this book are generic and apply to both primary and secondary teaching. Most of the illustrations and examples cited are from the appropriate phase of schooling, but in certain cases they are taken from another year group, either for the sake of clarity, or because the original research work referred to was done with that particular age cohort of pupils.

Unit 1   Why do we ask questions?

A 5-year-old girl returned from her first day at school and announced that her teacher was no good because she didn't know anything. When asked why she thought this, she replied that 'the teacher just kept on asking us things'. The implication behind her remark was that we normally ask questions when we really want to know something and, if you already know the answer, then you don't need to ask.

So why do teachers, and, for that matter, parents as well, ask children so many questions as part of the younger generation's induction into the knowledge, skills, values and culture of their forebears? Why do they not simply tell them all they need to know? Surely that would save a great deal of time.

As a preliminary to reading this unit, try tackling one or more of the following questions about questions.

Activity 1

Write down your answers to, or think about, the following three questions. In each case try to imagine one or two questions that people are likely to ask in the circumstances described.

1   'Why do *people* generally ask each other questions in daily conversation?'
2   'Why do *teachers* ask questions in their lessons?'
3   'Why do *pupils* ask questions in class, of one another, or of the teacher?'

Discuss your responses with fellow teachers or students, if you are a member of a group.

If you look at the answers and hypothetical questions you have thought of in the first category in Activity 1, people in general, you will see many different reasons lying beneath them. Some cover knowledge that a person might need in some aspect of daily life ('How do you mend a puncture?'). Others might be related to personal feelings and emotions ('Why are you upset?'). There are also

Why do teachers ask questions?

social reasons for asking questions in conversations ('How are you?'). We seek information or the solution to problems; we want to satisfy our curiosity or allay anxiety; we want to make contact with, or deepen our understanding of another person. There are numerous other reasons. Dillon (1994) is one of several writers who have explored the use of questions to stimulate thinking and discussion in classrooms.

WHY DO TEACHERS ASK QUESTIONS?

Teachers' reasons for asking questions of their pupils in classrooms are often rather different from those in everyday conversation. Put another way, the rules of talk in the classroom are different from those in other contexts. We often ask questions of children, not to obtain new knowledge for ourselves but to find out what children already know. This principle is stressed by Ausubel (1978):

> The most important single factor influencing learning is what the learner already knows. Ascertain this and teach him/her accordingly.

Other reasons for asking questions are to stimulate recall, to deepen understanding, to develop imagination and to encourage problem solving. There are also questions to do with class management, such as, 'Have you got your books?'. Turney *et al.* (1973), in their first edition of the Sydney Micro Series, list twelve possible functions of questions (see below).

Why do we ask questions?

To arouse interest and curiosity concerning a topic.
To focus attention on a particular issue or concept.
To develop an active approach to learning.
To stimulate pupils to ask questions of themselves and others.
To structure a task in such a way that learning will be maximised.
To diagnose specific difficulties inhibiting pupil learning.
To communicate to the group that involvement in the lesson is expected, and that overt participation by all members of the group is valued.
To provide an opportunity for pupils to assimilate and reflect upon information.
To involve pupils in using an inferred cognitive operation on the assumption that this will assist in developing thinking skills.
To develop reflection and comment by pupils on the responses of other members of the group, both pupils and teachers.
To afford an opportunity for pupils to learn vicariously through discussion.

Some reasons for asking questions

Source: Turney *et al.* (1973)

Turney's list is rather more comprehensive than that of most young teachers who are, for the first time, considering the way they ask questions of pupils. For example, in a study of 190 teachers in US elementary schools (primary schools), Pate and Bremer (1967) asked teachers to provide reasons for asking questions.

They found that the most common category was 'questions to check knowledge and understanding', followed by 'diagnosing pupils' difficulties' and 'recall of facts'. Only 10 per cent stressed the use of questions to encourage pupils to think. Significantly, there were no responses suggesting that questions may be used to help pupils to learn from each other, or that questions may be used to encourage pupils themselves to ask questions. Yet when teaching is discussed amongst professional people, encouraging pupils to talk and think is often stated as a high priority.

WHY DO TEACHERS ASK SPECIFIC QUESTIONS?

As well as thinking to oneself, 'Why do I ask questions in teaching?' it is also instructive to reflect on why a specific question is being asked, and indeed, why this specific question is being put to a particular individual or group. In one of our research projects we studied the reasons given by forty teachers (Brown and Edmondson, 1989). The results are shown below. In effect, the system is a summary of the reasons given by the teachers; it is not a set of mutually exclusive categories. The most common reasons were: encouraging thought, checking understanding, gaining attention, revision and management.

Encouraging thought, understanding of ideas, phenomena, procedures and values	33
Checking understanding, knowledge and skills	30
Gaining attention to task, to enable teacher to move towards teaching point in the hope of eliciting a specific and obscure point, as a warm-up activity for pupils	28
Review, revision, recall, reinforcement of recently learned point, reminder of earlier procedures	23
Management, settling down, to stop calling out by pupils, to direct attention to teacher or text, to warn of precautions	20
Specifically to teach whole class through pupil answers	10
To give everyone a chance to answer	10
Ask bright pupils to encourage others	4
To draw in shyer pupils	4
Probe children's knowledge after critical answers, redirect question to pupils who asked or to other pupils	3
To allow expressions of feelings, views and empathy	3

Reasons for asking specific questions (percentages of responses in each category)

The teachers who provided samples of questions they asked high-ability pupils cited 'gaining attention' and 'understanding' as their most frequent reason. Teachers of medium-ability classes reported more 'checking' and 'revision' questions, whereas teachers of low-ability groups tended to stress 'understanding' and 'management'. Teachers of mixed-ability classes favoured a wider range: 'understanding', 'gaining attention to move towards teaching point', 'management' and 'revision'.

There were differences between teachers of different subjects. Among the secondary English teachers in the sample, the most common reasons given were to gain attention and for management purposes, whereas the mathematics and science teachers gave priority to checking understanding and encouraging thought. Expressive arts and foreign language teachers gave more revision and checking reasons, whereas history and geography teachers provided more encouraging understanding and gaining attention reasons. The evidence suggests that the context is very important. Teachers' reasons for asking questions, not surprisingly, vary according to the subject or topic being taught, the class and the ability of the pupils.

In one of our research studies of questions asked by teachers in primary schools (Wragg, 1993), we asked them to identify three key questions and to discuss why they had chosen them. The questions that the teachers judged most successful very often provided a reason that contained a sense of looking ahead – the intention behind the question was evident. The least successful questions seemed to be looking nowhere, or were focused almost entirely upon what the children knew already. Perhaps most importantly of all, in the successful lessons, the key questions were related to the expressed aims of the lesson.

Another of our studies (Wragg, 1993) involved recording more than a thousand questions asked by primary teachers. The questions asked were divided into three categories: *managerial* if they were to do with the running of the lesson (e.g. 'Who's finished all the problems?'), *information/data* if they involved the recall of information (e.g. 'How many legs does an insect have?'), and *higher order* if pupils had to do more than just remember facts, for example, if they had to analyse, make generalisations or infer (e.g. 'Why is a bird not an insect?'). Here are some of the distributions obtained, given in percentages:

Target of question		Type of question	
Whole class	22	Managerial	57
Small groups	12	Information/data	35
Individuals	66	Higher order	8
Total	100	Total	100

There is no strong research evidence that one form of question is *invariably* 'better' than another, irrespective of context, but what observations would you make about the distributions given above? Suppose this were the distribution in your own lessons, would you want to make changes? If so, of what kind and why? And how would you achieve them?

We also analysed the distribution of questions in both categories combined, in order to see what types of questions were asked in what context. Here are the results, in descending order of frequency, so that the most common occurrence was 'managerial questions to individuals' (37 per cent), and the least common was 'higher-order questions to small groups' (1 per cent):

managerial to individuals	37
information/data to individuals	24
managerial to whole class	12
information/data to whole class	8
managerial to small groups	8
higher order to individuals	5
information/data to small groups	3
higher order to whole class	2
higher order to small groups	1
total	100

Suppose a teacher decided that she was spending too much time asking managerial questions of individuals and wanted to invest more effort in asking them to think more deeply about the subject matter of what they were learning, how might she set about this? Think in particular about class management (see *Class Management in the Secondary School* in this series), and how pupils might become more independent.

WHY DO PUPILS ASK QUESTIONS?

Children may ask a lot of questions – but not usually in school. Indeed, in one of our detailed analyses of questioning in twenty lessons (Wragg, 1993) there were fewer than twenty questions asked spontaneously by pupils and most of these questions were not centrally concerned with thinking.

Many questions asked by pupils of their teachers seem to be procedural, such as, 'What time do we finish?', 'Should we put the date?', rather than to do with the thinking processes involved in the subject matter, such as, 'Why is the sky blue?' or, 'What happens if … ? Teachers often remember the teasing or penetrating question asked by a pupil, but they are not necessarily all that frequent in occurrence. Similarly, the questions asked by pupils of each other are often on procedural or social matters, rather than to do with the subject content, unless their teacher specifically encourages them to ask questions. Swiss psychologist Jean Piaget's well-known adage (Piaget and Inhelder, 1969) that, 'All logical thinking arises out of the manipulation of objects' could well be extended to 'and the asking of questions'.

In addition to procedures and subject matter there are other reasons why pupils ask questions of the teacher or of each other. Often these will be related to the child's own emotional needs: for reassurance, attention, affection, or recog-

Why do pupils ask questions?

nition of achievement. Most time-consuming of these is probably attention-seeking, and the teacher may have to explore the reasons underlying attention-seeking by a particular pupil – always bearing in mind the needs of other pupils who are not so demanding in their quest for attention.

PURPOSES AND REASONS

The underlying purpose and reason for asking questions is both simple and complex. Put simply, questions are asked to facilitate learning, so they are linked to the aims of lessons and the underlying purpose of the lesson. The complexity increases as we unfold the purposes and we become aware of a myriad of reasons for asking questions and for asking specific questions of specific pupils.

The reasons for asking questions are closely related to the types of question asked – *cognitive* (knowledge and understanding), *affective* (to do with the emotions), *social and procedural* – or in terms of immediate *short-term and long-term goals*. As well as asking questions of pupils, teachers often, subconsciously, ask questions of themselves. These questions can be implicit, built into the structure of the activity being devised, or explicit, when they prepare lessons or topics ('What shall we do as a follow-up exercise to this activity?'), or when they evaluate their own performance as teachers ('Did it go well?', 'What could I have done better?'). Key questions should be linked to aims, for in so doing questions provide logic and structure for teachers as well as for pupils.

Activity 2

(If you do nothing else, try to do number 6 below and save the recording)

1   Look back at your answers to the three questions given in Activity 1. Add any points that you have discovered or rediscovered in this unit.

2   Why do pupils ask so few questions? List the possible reasons and choose the most important reasons. If you are in a group, compare your choices with those of colleagues.

3   What implications do these reasons have for organising your classroom and your teaching?

4   Thinking about questioning is not something that should be the exclusive preserve of teachers. It is worth finding a little time with a class to discuss the question, 'Why do people ask questions?' You might ask them to list the kinds of questions that one could ask about an object, or to produce a picture that provokes questions. A useful everyday topic for this activity is purchasing some new clothes, or buying someone a present. You might also ask them to develop a set of 'what', 'how' and 'why' questions about an object. You might also invite them to offer reasons why teachers and pupils ask questions in lessons, and how they themselves behave in this respect.

5   Read the following transcript and note and highlight your responses to these issues:

- Identify some managerial questions.
- Are all managerial questions really questions? Or are some really commands?
- Identify the first key question on what is to be the content of the lesson.
- Why do you think the teacher asked the key question?
- Was the next sequence of the lesson appropriate?
- Look at and analyse the pupils' responses.
- How would you have changed this sequence and lesson?

T: Right! Can you all sit down please and make a start? I'm sorry about the delay, but I think we're all together now. Can I have you all looking this way? Put everything down. Can you remember back to the end of last half term we did some work together on some creative writing with the title 'Spring', and today a small group of us will develop that work? … I want you to listen to the music and if you want to close your eyes you can if it helps you to concentrate, and just allow the music to bring up into your mind lots of ideas, lots of images. Now perhaps before we actually listen to the music I wonder if we could predict what this music will be like. The subject is going to be spring, let's write that up. I don't think you've heard this before. I haven't played it to you anyway. What do you imagine the music might be like? Claire?

P: Bouncy?

T: Right, bouncy music, OK, any other words? Fast? Anybody else? Why did you suggest those two words, for example?

P: Because of bouncing lambs in meadows.

T: Right, lambs bouncing around, springy, yes! When we think of spring as the season, what immediately comes into your mind first of all?

P: Flowers.

T: Flowers, good.

P: Sun.

T: Sun!

P: Animals.

T: Animals – what sort of animals?

P: Sheep.

T: Sheep, birds in the air?

P: New animals!

T: Right! New-born baby animals because what festival is there at springtime?

P: Easter.

T: Right! Easter and Easter is a time of what?

P: Joy and sorrow …

T: To begin with, what I would like you to do is just listen to it. Remember it's about spring; it's the beginning of life. At the beginning of the music I want you to remember you're coming out of winter, you're coming out of darkness, you're coming out of deadness if you like, into new life, sounds of the flute, birds' delight, day and night, nightingale in the dale, gale in the dale, lark in skies merrily, merrily. 'Little boy full of joy, little girl small and sweet, pop does crow, so do you, merry voice, instant noise, very merrily do we come to school, little lamb here I am, piping down the valley wild piping songs of pleasant dreams, piper sit thee down and write a book that all may read and then you vanished from my sight and I plucked a hollow reed and I made a rural pen and I stained the water clear!'

Now while the music's playing I just want you to think back on all the images that the music is bringing to mind. What I am going to do in a moment or two is give out large sheets of paper and in the groups where you are, rather like before, I want you to write down – you can talk together among yourselves, perhaps one person can write down the suggestions and the others can talk about it – all the different musical images that this music on spring conjures up …

Right! I'll start the music …

6   Prepare and teach a brief interactive lesson to your class. Make a video- or audio-recording of the lesson *and save it for subsequent analysis when you have finished this book (see Activity 16)*. Before reading the next unit, listen to or watch your tape and make freehand notes on the sorts of questions you asked in the lesson.

Unit 2 What kinds of questions do we ask?

In this unit we explore the kinds of questions that teachers ask their pupils and examine how those questions may be classified. We then offer some activities and suggestions to help you to reflect upon approaches to questioning, including your own.

STUDIES OF QUESTIONING

If you have been teaching for between five and ten years then you probably have asked from a quarter to half a million questions in your classes. Teachers with over fifteen years' experience may have asked a million questions. Even student teachers spending, say, ten weeks in a school teaching half a timetable, may well ask some five to ten thousand questions.

This rather startling conclusion is based on some remarkably stable evidence, reported throughout the last century, that teachers asked on average one or two questions every minute, sometimes more for certain activities; that most were to do with class management and the recall of factual information; that relatively few required higher-order thinking. Teachers of modern languages, for example, may well ask several questions per minute during the rapid-fire oral phases of lessons, but most involve simple answers to uncomplicated questions in the foreign language.

In an analysis of typescripts of lessons early last century, Stevens (1912) reported that teachers appeared to ask four hundred questions per day; that 65 per cent of those questions were concerned with recall of textbook information; that learning consisted mostly of responding to teacher questions and that virtually no questions asked by pupils were concerned directly with learning. Twenty-three years later, Haynes (1935) discovered that 70 per cent of questions that teachers asked 12–13-year-olds required factual answers and only 17 per cent fostered pupils' thinking. In his 1970 review of teachers' questions, Gall noted that 60 per cent of teacher questions required pupils to recall facts in much the same way as that in which they were presented, and only 20 per cent required pupils to think beyond a level of recall; the remaining 20 per cent involved procedural matters such as classroom management. Other writers provide similar but slightly different percentages and Galton, Simon and Kroll (1980) in their study of primary and middle schools report that only 12 per cent of teaching time was devoted to questions: of this 29 per cent was devoted to factual questions, 23 per cent to ideas, and more than 47 per cent to tasks of provision and routine management. Kerry (1989) analysed the questions teachers asked in 213 hours of lessons in RE, French, history, mathematics, English, geography and music in five secondary schools. He found that 54 per cent were about management, 42 per cent involved information and only 4 per cent stimulated a higher order of thinking. This 54 – 42 – 4 percentage split for secondary lessons is astonishingly close to the 57 – 35 – 8 finding for primary classrooms reported above (Wragg, 1993).

The evidence on frequency of questions is not a good guide to pupil achievement. Correlations between question frequency and achievement are weak. Indeed, one writer (Dillon, 1981) argues that excessive questioning makes pupils dependent and passive. Too much questioning can evoke anxiety and too little may mute thought. There is division of opinion in the research literature about the extent to which types of questions asked are related to pupil achievement. Higher-order (thought) questions do promote thinking and lower-order (factual) questions do promote the recall of facts. Indeed, the whole issue of 'higher' and 'lower' order thinking is itself quite contentious, a matter we discuss in more detail in the companion book in this series *Explaining in the Secondary School*. The only conclusion that can be drawn from this is that you have to choose what kinds of learning you want to promote, and then choose appropriate types of questions. This conclusion is particularly important when teachers are laying the foundations of understanding in science, mathematics and the arts.

Barnes and Todd (1977) showed that pupils who worked in small discussion groups, without the teacher present, generated more exploratory questions, hypotheses and explanations than when teachers were present. Using slightly different perspectives, Edwards and Furlong (1978) described their investigations of traditional classrooms in terms of the teacher's authority and control of knowledge, where the teacher provided a framework into which pupil talk is fitted and that talk is assessed according to the closeness of fit.

TYPES OF QUESTIONS

There are many ways of categorising questions, some of which we shall now explore. The content of many questions that are to do with learning a particular subject, rather than procedural issues, may be classified as predominantly one of three types:

1   *Conceptual questions* concerned with eliciting ideas, definitions and reasoning in the subject being studied.
2   *Empirical questions* requiring answers based on facts or on experimental findings.

3   *Value questions* investigating relative worth and merit, moral and environmental issues.

These broad categories of the content of questions often overlap and they are by no means clear-cut. Some questions, particularly key questions, may involve elements of all three types of questions.

This classification of questions may seem, at first sight, remote from teaching pupils in school and more akin to work in universities. Yet, given the importance of laying foundations in the sciences and arts, it follows that these questions are likely to be found, in some form or other, at all levels in classes in the primary and secondary school. As well as types of questions, there are dimensions of questioning. These are discussed in the next section.

Conceptual questions

In studying the classification of animals, it is not unusual for a teacher to ask pupils to assemble their own taxonomy, to sort the animals they can think of into different groups, according to their own criteria, and then look at 'official' taxonomies. If members of the class are then asked questions like, 'Why have you put *cats* and *dogs* in the same category?', 'What do you call animals with and without bones?' or, 'This animal lays eggs, so why have you put it into the *mammals* group?', then these would all be conceptual questions, aimed at helping the pupil grasp some of the key features, like *vertebrate/invertebrate*, of an animal taxonomy. The process of thinking about correct and incorrect answers should help pupils formulate, or clarify the relevant concepts.

Empirical questions

Empirical types of questions involve observation, recall of facts and possible experimentation. If reasoning is used, it is to confirm the facts or to show the connections between the facts and observations. Here are two examples drawn from the transcripts from lessons observed during research projects. This first is from a lesson about forces, the second is about the skin and how it helps animals to avoid drying out. Notice how the teachers concerned structure their empirical questions, helping pupils to observe, speculate, connect one fact with another. Look out for amplifications of the question (e.g. using some kind of demonstration or visual aid, giving hints in the question or the preamble about what to look for, summarising, using pupils' ideas).

Transcript 1

T: When I blew up the balloon, Sarah said that the air presses against the side of the cup and lifts the cup up with the balloon. So what do you think is going to happen if I let go of the cup?

P: It's going to stay.

T: It's going to stay with the balloon. What if I start to let go of the balloon?

P: It will fall off.

P: All the air will start coming out and friction on the side of the cup will start letting go, so then the friction will stop and then it will fall off.

T: Gosh! We've got another word in here – friction! – say it again, really loud this time.

P: Well, when the air goes out the friction will kind of come off the cup and then the friction will let go of the cup and then the cup will drop off.

T: Right! So Jonathan is saying that there is some friction holding the balloon and the cup and that when the air comes out of the balloon, the cup is going to drop off – does anybody else think that the cup's going to drop off? Who's not sure? Be honest, it doesn't matter what you think. So if I let go of it – the cup drops to the floor – right, OK, so you've got some cups in front of you and you've got four balloons, so you can try it. Now what have you got to do when you're doing it?

P: Don't let the air out!

T: Don't let the air out, keep it in, right. Let's have a look at Rebecca's because she's got her balloon up quite a long way.

Transcript 2

T: There are a lot of animals that don't stay in water all their life, aren't there? Can you think of how they— If you think of a sponge and we're saying it can't stay in water all the time – can you think of how we could stop it from drying out?

P: Put water on it now and again.

T: We could put water on it now and again. Can you think of any other ideas? What could we do to the sponge to stop it drying out? Supposing you wanted to take a sponge away with you on holiday and you wanted it wet 'cos you weren't sure whether you were going to get any water. What would you do with it? Yes?

P: Wrap it up in something.

T: You'd wrap it up in something. Yes. What sort of thing can you think you'd wrap it up in? Yes?

P: Polythene.

T: Yes. We could put it in a polythene bag. There we are [produces polythene bag and puts sponge in it], there's a polythene bag. Now, animals, well, we don't have polythene round us, do we? But we do have things round us to stop us drying up. We have our skin, don't we?

Value questions

Value questions are concerned with morals, social concerns such as poverty, health issues such as smoking, and environmental issues such as pollution. They can occur in lessons on personal, social and health education, religious education, citizenship, preparation for adult life, or other lessons and topics where values, behaviour and beliefs are being discussed. They may also occur in lessons on literature, history, geography, science, technology – indeed, in any lesson where what people believe, or what is thought to be right and wrong, is being investigated.

Activity 3

This transcript is taken from a class discussion about poverty in old age. It ranges across several issues and involves questions about different aspects of how people behave, what values inform behaviour and beliefs and the causes of misfortune. Read through it and pick out a few questions concerned with values, ideas and the exploration of such 'facts' as exist in discussions about beliefs. Questions about matters of belief and behaviour can touch on very sensitive issues, so look in particular at how the teacher responds to pupils' contributions.

Transcript 3

T: We want to think particularly today of some of the problems of old people. Now of course we could equally talk about their happiness. Not all old people are sad, but because we want talk about communities later on, we want to focus on their problems. I have put a poem on the board; it's only a fairly brief one. I want you to have a look at this poem and at the end of that I want you to tell me something about the problem of this man as represented in the poem. [Uncovers poem written on blackboard.] Perhaps someone would like to read it to us before we start to talk about it. Bruce, would you like to?

P: If you go there just before it is dark,
    If you go to the park, the wind blows and the leaves cling to the fences and the papers fly,
    He sits there on the seat by the track an old, old man;
    A fag in his lips, brown teeth, white hair and a wet chin.

T: All right, now, what about that man, what are some of the problems you think he might face? – Linda.

P: He sounds as if he is very old.

T: Yes.

P: And he's got nothing left.

T: All right, that's a good answer.

P: I think that he's poor and he's just sitting in the park on a brisk day and he's remembering about his childhood.

T: Why do you say he's poor – what makes you have that impression?

P: Oh, just the whole poem just gives you the impression that he's poor.

T: All right, we'll put that up on the board in a moment – Stephen.

P: And I think he is an old tramp because we find lots of them in our parks round the community.

T: Good.

P: And quite a few of these people don't shave and they drink methylated spirits and things like that.

T: All right, there are a lot of factors that you have told us. Now why do you think people might drink methylated spirits? Why do they sit around in the park all day – James?

P: Because they haven't got a home or if they have it's not much of a home and it's too expensive to try to buy beer or whisky or anything like that, so it's pretty cheap to buy methylated spirits.

T: Good, we're coming back to this point up here, aren't we? Somebody said that this man was poor and you are saying that they buy methylated spirits because beer is too dear. There's one word that I am thinking of, they lack lots of what?

P: Education.

> *T:* Well, education is one thing that we can come to in a moment.
> *P:* They might be lonely and they look at all the birds and things to pass the time.
> *T:* All right, these are very good answers but there is one word that I want us to get up here. [Points to the space near the word 'Poor'.] There are lots of things that go together because they lack what? Lots of?
> *P:* Money.
> *T:* Money! Right! I'm thinking of ordinary old money …
> *P:* They are probably very lonely and they go to the park and watch all the birds and just think back, and they think how lovely nature is and how the city is being destroyed and all that.

DIMENSIONS OF QUESTIONS

Closely related to the matter of *type* of question is the issue of *dimension*. A conceptual type of question, for example, could be described on several dimensions, often expressed in opposites such as 'narrow/broad', or 'confused/clear'. A narrow or closed version might be, 'Is a bee an insect?', to which there is a correct one-word answer – 'yes' – verifiable in a textbook. A more broad or open conceptual question on the same topic might be, 'What do you know about insects?'

Given the range and frequency of questions that pupils are asked, it is well worth giving a little thought to some of the more important dimensions. As was indicated earlier, there are several ways of classifying questions, so we will concentrate on a few dimensions that teachers have found useful when reflecting on the range and nature of questions that they ask of their pupils.

The narrow/broad (often referred to as the 'closed/open') dimension

Questions may be framed to require a relatively brief, specific answer (for example, 'What is the capital of France?') or to require a relatively wide-ranging set of possibilities (like, 'What can be done to combat crime?'). These questions may be represented as points on a dimension, although you should bear in mind that a narrow question in one context ('What do you need to get into a house?') may be a broad question in another ('What do you need to get into heaven?'). The narrow/broad dimension of questions is sometimes described as closed/open or convergent/divergent.

Not surprisingly, excessive use of narrow questions yields short answers and frequently inhibits discussion. Sometimes the form of a broad question is used, yet the teacher is nonetheless searching for a single specific answer. A football coach once asked a group of players, 'What do you never do in the penalty area?' to which the expected answer was, 'Pass the ball across the face of the goal', but the range of possible answers was mind-boggling. Such pseudo-broad questions can evoke frustration rather than information if pupils suspect that the teacher is merely fencing for a single preferred answer, rather than appealing to the imagination. In one study, more than 50 per cent of this type of question failed to receive any answers from pupils, so the teachers often answered their own questions (Barnes, 1969).

The observation/recall/thought dimension

This dimension is perhaps the most difficult to grasp. Recall and observation are intimately related in children. It has been part of their growing up to learn to match a fresh observation against previous experiences, to help grasp its significance or place it in the scheme of things. Put another way, none of us can observe or describe a new observation without recourse to prior experiences and ideas, for how else would we be able to use the right vocabulary, or explain its significance and relationship to other events and phenomena?

However, the recall of facts can, of course, occur in the absence of fresh observation of them, as we have developed, since childhood, a greater permanence to our memory that is not dependent on a visual stimulus. In turn, the recall of facts, or previously known ideas, can influence and condition our observations and also provide the basis for thinking. If we see a tree, a bird, or a motor car, we recall similar or identical examples to help us classify and code our new observation. That is why many teachers begin their lessons with a request for a recall ('Can anyone remember ...?') or for observation ('What do you notice about ...?'). Broadly speaking, 'recall' questions test existing knowledge and observation, whereas 'thought' questions use old knowledge to create new knowledge and ideas in the learner.

Recall questions are often used in the initial or early stages of a lesson, so that the teacher can assess knowledge and starting points, and also start up and focus children's thinking processes. However, one danger of this approach is that the pupils may be puzzled if the questions seem too simple and self-evident, or they may simply become bored and begin to behave disruptively if revision and recall seem endless.

As indicated earlier, our study of more than one thousand teachers' questions showed only eight per cent of these required higher-order thinking, involving children in going beyond the mere recall of facts. There are several reasons for this; one particularly important reason is that teachers do not necessarily prepare such questions, but somehow expect them to arise spontaneously. It may be that if we want to ask questions that get children to think, then we have to think about the questions that we are going to ask them.

The dimension of recall/thought is sometimes confused with the narrow/broad dimension. Yet it is clear that some questions can be 'narrow thought' questions, such as, 'Are there more insects in the world than there are beetles?'. This is a closed question, but one which requires a little logical reasoning. They can also be 'narrow recall' questions, like, 'What date was the battle of Hastings?' Some may be 'broad recall' questions: for example, 'What have we learned about human responses to the effects of earthquakes?' and some may be 'broad thought' questions: for example, 'How can unemployment be reduced in our society?'

Certain higher-order or thought questions can yield a large number of responses from pupils, particularly when the higher-order questions are broad.

Body language

Such questions may also lead to greater gains in understanding and to pupils evaluating teaching more positively, though the research evidence is divided on this. It should also be borne in mind, when reflecting on or using the recall/thought dimension, that what an 11-year-old may require to think afresh, may only require a 15-year-old to recall.

The confused/clear dimension

Clear questions are usually brief, direct and firmly anchored in the context of the lesson. The choice of language is precise, to cut down on ambiguity. Confusion is often generated by questions buried in a set of other statements, or, even worse, in other questions, so that the pupil is not sure which question is being asked. Sometimes the confusion arises if a key term has not been explained first. One mathematics teacher, for example, confused the class by asking, 'How could we draw a stratified random sample from a population if we wanted to study, say, levels of income?' Although the class knew what a 'random sample' was, he had not explained what 'stratified' meant in this context. Other examples of common errors in this type of questioning are given in Unit 3, when we discuss tactics.

The encouraging/threatening dimension

Voice, gesture, body language, humour, smiles, frowns, are all important aspects of asking questions, sometimes known as *non-verbal*, or *paralinguistic* features, because they go with the words that are used. The same question may

Activity 4 Analysing your questions

The following table sets out a simple system based upon the dimensions of questions that may be used to analyse your questions. Management and procedural questions are omitted in this analysis of your teaching. The system is easiest to use on a sample of the questions that you ask. First, write down a sample as you are listening to an audio or videotape of your own lesson or someone else's, and then analyse the questions. Two or three colleagues could work together on this and then analyse and compare their lessons. In using the system, bear in mind the ages and abilities of the pupils, as well as the nature of the subject matter you are teaching. As indicated earlier, one pupil's 'thought' may be another's 'recall'. Last but not least, don't expect to agree on the dimensions of every single question sampled.

Questions	Dimensions								
	Recall	Obser-vation	Thought	Broad	Narra-tive	Confused	Clear	Encour-aging	Threat-ening

This 'Ask it' system of analysis is designed to help you to classify the questions asked while teaching a class, group or individual. Simply note down a sample of the questions asked, from a tape-recording of a lesson, classify each question on each dimension and examine the pattern of questions asked.

be asked in a variety of ways, which encourage or inhibit pupil responses, using emphasis for effect, 'Don't you know the *answer*?' (kindly, smiling, willing to help) or, 'Don't you *know* the answer?' (angry, menacing, with an unspoken 'you complete idiot' in brackets).

Teachers' questions are usually intended to include, rather than exclude, to help pupils think and contribute to discussion, rather than frighten them into silence, so an encouraging mode of questioning and responding is probably more effective than a threatening tone. This is not to say that questions should not confront or challenge, but the right timbre of voice, turn of phrase and accompanying demeanour can turn a perceived threat into an acceptable challenge.

Activity 4 will help you to identify different kinds of questions. It helps you to become more aware of the questions that you ask and it can help you to improve your use of questions in class. Simply put a tick in any column whenever it seems appropriate. For example, the teacher may ask the question, 'Is the ball floating or sinking?' You might decide this is 'observation', because the child must look; 'narrow' because the answer is 'yes' or 'no'; 'clear', as it refers to a specific object the child can see before him; and neither 'encouraging' nor 'threatening', so you would leave that dimension blank. On the other hand, if the question were, 'Why is the ball sinking?' some of your choices might be different, as more complex thought processes are involved and pupils might need to know about 'buoyancy' and 'density'.

Activity 5

1   Read the following transcripts of two lessons in which the teachers ask a series of questions, then classify them using the 'Ask it' system of analysis, (except for the encouraging/threatening dimension, which you cannot judge from a transcript alone). Compare your analysis with those of colleagues, if possible. In so doing, look not only at the questions, but the pattern, if any, in the sequence of questions asked.

Transcript 4

The lesson was on Shakespeare's play *Julius Caesar*, on the scene where both Brutus and Mark Antony address the crowd after Caesar has been killed.

T: So what's the mood of the crowd after Brutus has addressed them?
P: Ugly.
T: What do you mean, 'ugly'?
P: They're on his side, they think he was right to kill Julius Caesar.
T: Fine. So what sort of reception does Mark Antony get?
P: Nobody listens when he first starts to speak. He has to shout for them to be quiet.
P: And he has to work hard to turn them round.
T: Turn them round?
P: Get them on his side.
T: OK, so the crowd are very hostile, but he changes their mood completely. How?
P: He tells them what a great man Caesar was.
T: What, right at the beginning?
P: No, he says, 'I come to bury Caesar, not to praise him' to get them quiet. Then he gradually gets more sarcastic about Brutus.

T: How does he do that?

P: He keeps saying, 'Brutus was an honourable man', but then he tells them all about the good things Caesar has done.

T: Like what?

P: Like leaving them all some money in his will.

Transcript 5

This lesson was on the question, 'Why is it that birds can fly?' The extract is taken from the fourth minute into the lesson.

T: How big are your muscles, David? Where are your muscles?

P: Here. [Pointing.]

P: Everywhere.

T: What are muscles for?

P: To make sure you can move.

T: How do they work?

P: If you don't have any muscles you'd just be flab and if you've got muscles then you can jump around and all that.

T: Very good, thank you very much, John – now we've got a picture of it – find this muscle here and rest your hand on top of it. [Puts hand on bicep.]

P: Mine can go really high!

T: How do you make it go really high then, John?

P: You've just got to flex it up and turn it round.

T: … so do you think bird muscles are actually bigger than that?

P: No.

T: I think they've got more muscles than us though.

P: Yes, because they're smaller and they can fit more in.

T: What do you think, Luke?

P: If you're bigger, then you might get a bit more than if you're smaller.

T: So, if you've got more muscles you are bigger – you'll have to think about that one and find out a bit more about it. Yes, Adam?

P: The humming bird is small, so he can go really fast and he's lighter.

T: Do you think that that helps him fly – the fact that he's lighter?

P: Yes …

2   Now think of a topic that you are going to teach. Write down a sample of ten questions that you might possibly ask your pupils, should the opportunity arise. Then classify them using the narrow/broad, recall/observation/thought and clear/confused dimensions. If working with colleagues, exchange questions (but not your classifications) with someone else and then classify each other's questions. Compare and discuss your classifications. Now consider if and how some of the questions could be improved. Discuss what sort of response you would expect each question to get from your class, and then teach your lesson. See what response you actually obtain, as well as how accurate you were in your guesses about the impact of the questions.

Unit 3 What are the tactics of effective questioning?

> No one can teach, if by teaching we mean the transmission of knowledge, in any mechanical fashion, from one person to another. The most that can be done is that one person who is more knowledgeable than another can, by asking a series of questions, stimulate the other to think, and so cause him to learn for himself.
>
> Socrates, fifth century BC

Socrates destroyed the arguments of his opponents by asking them a series of questions, thus exposing the inconsistencies in their thinking. For him the final stage of education was liberation, when the pupil, through questioning, finally rejected habit and prejudice. His name has often been attached to the general strategy of teaching by asking a series of questions, known as *the Socratic method*.

Thinking about effective teaching goes back a long way in history and Socrates is one of many thinkers in classical Europe, China, India and elsewhere who spoke and wrote about teaching tactics. In China, in the fifth century BC, Confucius also sought the liberation, rather than dependency, of his pupils, saying:

> In his teaching the wise man guides his students but does not pull them along; he urges them to go forward and does not suppress them; he opens the way but does not take them to the place; … if his students are encouraged to think for themselves we may call the man a good teacher.

Questions are only as good as the answers that they elicit, so it is important to consider not only the types of question that teachers ask, but also the tactics involved in asking those questions. One obvious purpose of effective questioning is to minimise teachers' and pupils' errors by focusing on a particular fact, issue, skill, belief, or whatever. Activity 6 invites you to reflect on the extent to which you agree or disagree with the following list of 'errors'.

- Asking too many questions at once.
- Asking a question and answering it yourself.
- Asking questions only of the brightest or most likeable pupils.
- Asking a difficult question too early in the sequence of events.
- Asking irrelevant questions.
- Always asking the same types of questions (e.g. closed ones).
- Asking questions in a threatening way.
- Not indicating a change in the type of question.
- Not using probing questions.
- Not giving pupils the time to think.
- Not correcting wrong answers.
- Ignoring pupils' answers.
- Failing to see the implications of pupils' answers.
- Failing to build on answers.

Some common 'errors' in questioning

Activity 6

1   Put a tick by any of the 'errors' given in the checklist above that you think you have committed within the last few weeks. Are they necessarily 'errors'? If you have been teaching, yet do not tick any item, then you do not need to read the rest of this section. On the other hand, if you are honest …

2   Compare your 'errors' with those of a few colleagues. Discuss how you might avoid committing those errors. What other errors in questioning do you have?

3   Teach and audio- or video-record a segment of a lesson (or invite a colleague to observe a lesson and sample the questions that you use). Use the checklist to identify and discuss anything that might arguably be regarded as an 'error' you have made. Reflect with your colleague how the questioning might have been improved.

KEY TACTICS

Among the key tactics involved when asking questions are:

1   Structuring;
2   Pitching and putting clearly;
3   Directing and distributing;
4   Pausing and pacing;
5   Prompting and probing;
6   Listening to replies and responding;
7   Sequencing.

Structuring (Signposting)

Structuring consists of providing *signposts* for the sequence of questions and the topic. The structuring may be a brief exposition of the topic, a review of a series of questions and explanations based on a previous lesson or a statement of objectives. Sometimes structuring moves are described as 'pre-formulators' (French and Maclure, 1983). Pre-formulators indicate the kinds of answers that the teacher expects, the clues being part of the question. French and Maclure use the term 'orientations' to describe deliberate attempts to build on pupils' previous knowledge and experience. Again, these are concerned with structuring.

In cognitive psychology, Ausubel (1978) uses the term 'advance organisers' to describe the activation and direction of pupils' learning to what is going to be studied (saying in effect, 'This is what we are going to do'). The important point is that structure with a well-defined initial focus is an essential tactic of effective questioning. We discuss more fully the use of 'advance organisers' in the companion book, *Explaining in the Secondary School*.

Activity 7   Examples of structuring

Two attempts at structuring, setting the scene for subsequent questions, are given in Transcripts 6 and 7. Neither is perfect. Consider how they could be improved.

Transcript 6

T: The thing about basketball is you've got to stop people getting the ball, if you can. So we're going to learn how to do a 'press'. You've got to close people down, pressure their space. In some sports you do zones, but with this you've got to go man to man. When you do the press you've got to threaten people so they give the ball away.

Transcript 7

T: Now, as I was saying, when I give *you* the clues, you give me *thinking*, when it gets to the last two clues I am pretty sure that everybody will know. Right, here we go, Number 1. John, are you listening? Now, the creature I am thinking of today has the ability … is able … to make at least twelve different sounds, right. Now think about that and don't say anything to anybody. This animal likes to live in groups of up to twelve or more. Don't put your hands up, I don't need it. I want you to be thinking in there. [Points to head.] This creature is a peaceful animal. He doesn't have many enemies; his main enemy, unfortunately, is man. [Clues continue in this way.]

'Pitching' and putting questions clearly – language register, choosing your words

The 'pitch and putt' analogy here is with the short golf course, where you chip the ball onto the green, as close to the hole as you can get it, and then roll it in with your putter. 'Pitching' in general conversation also refers to estimating the right intellectual level of the people you are teaching, so that you neither bewilder nor patronise them.

Choosing the right language register

In this context, the term refers to selecting appropriately the recall/thought and narrow/broad dimensions described in Unit 2. All four types of questions – narrow-recall, broad-recall, narrow-thought and broad-thought – should be used when pitching questions. Sometimes it may be necessary to pitch a variety of broad-recall questions, at other times you may want to use a narrow-thought question. Of course, you should bear in mind that what may be a difficult thought question for one pupil or class of pupils may be a self-evident banality to another individual or group.

The 'putting' analogy, rolling the golf ball neatly into the hole, refers to *language register* – that is, phrasing the question by using words and phrases that are appropriate to the individual pupil or group. Do you use the technical term 'inversely proportional' or do you resort to everyday language with 'the more you have of this, the less you have of that'? We discuss the matter of language in the companion book *Explaining in the Secondary School*, but it is a decision that doctors have to make every day with their patients: do they say 'upper respiratory infection' or 'common cold'? Pupils have to learn the correct terminology for different subjects in the curriculum at some time themselves, so they cannot and should not be shielded from technical expressions all the time, but knowing when to use what kind of language is a central skill in effective questioning.

A common error made during school experience by trainee postgraduate students is to ask questions in the language of their degree subject. They feel comfortable and secure with this language, but their pupils do not:

'What do you think an ecological succession is?'

Such questions, particularly when embedded in long rambling phrases containing even more of the language of technical expertise, are likely to confuse and generate problems of class control. Sometimes the question may be put clearly by focusing on the aspect that needs addressing, as in the following question. This has the effect of narrowing the choice:

'There is a society for King Charles the Martyr, but was Charles I a martyr, or a traitor?'

Being able to choose the most appropriate language register for the person who is being addressed is crucial here. You would probably ask undergraduates in a dental school, 'What is the aetiology of dental caries?' without hesitation, but a better choice of language for pupils studying health in school might be, 'Why do sweets rot your teeth?', though this does not rule out their learning the term 'dental caries' at a suitable moment.

Directing and distributing

'How many pupils answered questions during the oral phase of that lesson?' is a killer question to ask a teacher. 'Hard to say, it seemed pretty busy, about twenty to twenty-five was it?' was one reply we had in a lesson where we had tallied every pupil who had spoken. The figure we had obtained was actually eight pupils, mostly sitting in central seats, though there had often been twenty or more raised hands. There is a sizeable difference between the teacher's estimate of twenty to twenty-five and the eight who actually contributed. It is easy to deceive oneself about distributing questions in class.

Undirected questions often lead to chorus answers and lack of control. Hence the importance of directing questions, when this is appropriate, by name, gesture, head movement or facial expressions. Distributing questions around the group, rather than concentrating on one or two willing respondents, not only involves more pupils but also reduces the risk of losing attention and class control. Some teachers often subconsciously favour the approach of asking mainly knowledgeable pupils, if only because their answers come more quickly or seem more rewarding.

One method of distribution is to ask every pupil in the group in turn, something which teachers we have interviewed and observed during research projects did not usually favour, or, alternatively questions can be distributed randomly around the class. Certain parts of the room can get ignored by a new teacher, but also by experienced practitioners. Children sitting along the sides of a classroom may be overlooked when the teacher is standing in the centre at the front. Groups of pupils at the back may be ignored if a teacher is seated at a desk. It is worth considering where your blind spots are when distributing questions, otherwise most may be addressed to children sitting in a V-shaped wedge in front of the teacher. The handling of interactive teaching of this kind is discussed more fully in the companion book *Class Management in the Secondary School*.

Sometimes, in open class or individual interaction, a pupil makes a substantial point or provides an answer that requires further elaboration, so the teacher may need to store that answer or contribution and return to it at a later point. When a pupil's response contains an error it is often tempting to address the same question to someone else, but there is also the option to turn the question back to the same pupil, with or without giving him further assistance. This is particularly useful in modern language lessons when pupils mispronounce words, or utter something with poor intonation.

T: Was macht er?   (What is he doing?)

P: Er ... geht ... über ... die ... Brücke.   ('He's ... walking ... across ... the ... bridge', spoken slowly and hesitantly).

T: Noch einmal – 'Er geht über die Brücke'.   ('Again – he's walking across the bridge.' The teacher repeats the answer fluently and with expression.)

P: Er geht über die Brücke.   ('He's walking across the bridge.' The pupil replies much more fluently and expressively this time.)

T: Ja, sehr gut. ('Yes, very good.')

Part of the tactics of directing and distributing questions is monitoring the body language of the pupils. By looking at pupils you can often identify those who wish to contribute, those who are not attending and those who are puzzled. This then raises the question of whether teachers should only call on pupils whose hands are up. In our research studies of teacher attitudes to questioning most have been opposed to this tactic, also wanting the option to nominate those who are not expressing willingness to respond as well.

Pausing and pacing

Student teachers often ask more questions than they receive answers (Brown, 1978) and they sometimes answer their own queries. This failure may often be due to lack of pauses, absence of what an American researcher, Mary Budd Rowe, has called 'wait time' (Rowe, 1978). She analysed eight hundred tape recordings of lessons and found that teachers asked between three and five questions per minute, but allowed only a second or less for a child to respond before asking someone else, answering the question themselves, or rephrasing the question. When she persuaded teachers to extend the *wait time* to three seconds or more, not only after the teacher's question, but also after the child's response, she found that the quality and length of pupils' answers improved. Her findings are discussed in the companion book in this series *Explaining in the Secondary School*.

The testimony of experienced teachers and the studies reviewed by Tobin (1987) also show that pausing briefly after a question and after an answer encourages more pupils to answer, more of the pupils to provide longer answers and more questions from pupils. Some of these findings may be because teachers who use pauses also tend to use a wide variety of questions and vary the pace of questions. Pauses act as signals for pace. Drill questions can be asked quickly, whereas more complex questions require longer pauses. After all, if you want pupils to think before giving their answer, then you need to give them the time to do so. Sometimes deeper questions might even be asked at the end of a lesson, so that pupils have a long time to think – until the next lesson on that topic, 'Why do you think that … is the case? I'm not going to tell you the answer now, so think about it before tomorrow's lesson'. Very intriguing.

Prompting and probing

Prompts and probes are follow-up questions when the first answers are inadequate, or inappropriate. Prompts contain hints (e.g. 'Think back to what we learned about … '), while probes require more precise or detailed answers ('Tell me a bit more about … ', 'Can you give me an example … ?', 'What do you mean exactly by … ?') Clues to the answer may be contained in the question. Three forms of prompts are:

- Rephrasing the question in different, perhaps simpler, words that relate more closely to the pupil's knowledge and experience.
- Asking a sequence of simple questions that eventually lead back to the original question.
- Providing a review of information given so far and then asking questions that will help the pupil to recall or see the answer.

Probing questions are probably the most important tactic for developing the thinking of pupils. More examples are given below.

- Does that always apply?
- Can you give me an example of that?
- How does that fit in (relevance)?
- You say it is X, which particular kind of X? What are the exceptions?
- Why do you think that is true?
- Is there another view?
- What is the idea behind that?
- Can you tell me the difference between the two?

Examples of probing questions

Probing questions may be related to the encouraging/threatening dimension mentioned in Unit 2. If they are asked in an encouraging way, then they are providing a challenge and can even be fun. If asked in a threatening way, they can inhibit thinking and demotivate learning. Probing questions, if used insensitively, can lead to management problems. Intensive teacher questioning of one pupil can lead to pupil disruption, even if the line of questioning is gentle.

Teasing out the full answer from one pupil may cause other members of the class to lose interest.

Sometimes pupils may benefit from being able to consult each other, especially with more thought-provoking questions. Gall and Artero-Boneme (1994) describe the *Heads together* approach, which involves putting pupils into mixed ability groups of four. From time to time the teacher asks these groups, rather than individuals, to delve into the question asked and put their heads together to produce their best answers.

Listening to replies

Our capacity to listen diminishes with anxiety, so it is not surprising that sometimes teachers may not listen carefully to the responses of pupils and so do not respond appropriately to their answers and comments. Four types of listening may be identified:

Skim listening   This is little more than awareness that a pupil is talking and is often done when the answers seem irrelevant, when you want to get on with what you are doing, or are thinking of other matters.

Survey listening   Trying to build a wider mental map of what the pupil is talking about. The listener filters out extraneous material and identifies the key points or misunderstandings of the pupil. This tactic is particularly important with pupils who are learning fresh subject matter. At its core is the capacity to understand how children think and talk.

Search listening   Active searching for specific information to an answer, or to a series of answers. Although it is important to search, it is also important not to overlook other answers or responses, for they may reveal more than the original question did.

Study listening   A subtle blend of search and survey listening, which goes beyond the words that the pupils use to their underlying meaning and uncertainties. It simply is not possible, given the demands on teachers' awareness, to 'study listen' all the time to one's pupils. What is more important is to be aware of the level of listening which you are currently using.

Responding

Responding is the move you make after a pupil answers or comments. Responding moves are, in a sense, the linchpins of a lesson, because they establish, in the eyes of the pupil, the tone of the lesson, by signalling the teacher's enthusiasm, excitement, interest, boredom, or indifference to what pupils have to offer. They are important, therefore, in sequencing and structuring a lesson, the mechanisms whereby new information is introduced, the topic is changed, the discussion is moved on and the lesson is moved back on course. Responding moves are some of the most difficult tactics for newly qualified teachers to master. Some of the more common responding moves are shown opposite.

Effective responses include giving reinforcement and feedback to pupils. It is also associated with conveying enthusiasm and generating interest. There is a risk for beginners. Grateful for any response, they might, unwittingly, react positively to every answer, regardless of its merits. Reinforcement and feedback eventually become meaningless, as pupils realise that not all answers can be wonderful, so the structure and sequence of the lesson may be lost. The risk for experienced teachers is to respond in a mechanical way. Automatic smiles and uncritical approval lose the effect on pupils that more discriminating responses would achieve.

Answer/comment	Teacher response
ignored	asks someone else, changes question, changes topic
acknowledged	nods, smiles, says 'right' or 'yes'
repeated verbatim	merely re-states it, inflects voice to convert into question
part of answer echoed	merely re-states acceptable part, inflects voice to convert into question
paraphrased	paraphrases directly, sometimes in the form of a question
praise contribution	praises contribution, with elaboration
corrected	corrects incorrect part of answer, asks others to correct
prompted	asks prompting questions, or supplies direct hint to pupil
probe	asks probing questions of pupil, or of other pupils

Responding to answers and comments

Three important ways of conveying interest are:

1   To take a pupil's answer and build on it or invite other pupils to build on it – 'A spider's not an insect, that's right, Caroline. Can anyone think why people believe a spider's an insect when it isn't really?
2   To refer to a previous contribution from a pupil and to link it to the present contribution, thereby showing the connections between the pupil's own contributions and the topic under discussion – 'Now, Peter's told us that the magnet picked up the paper clip and Sally said it wouldn't pick up a brass curtain ring, so what does a magnet pick up?'
3   To incorporate the pupil's contributions (by name) into summaries and reviews of what has been learned in the lesson – 'So Jacky's guess was right. People who eat more sweets do have more fillings, because things you eat can affect your body.'

One teacher we observed had a most engaging way of responding, which was clearly part of his deep structures of teaching that he had laid down over many years. He would make sure that pupils' replies were challenged intellectually, always in a friendly, if slightly adversarial way. Pupils enjoyed this spirited style, for it was never unkind or sarcastic, but it made them think carefully, as this lively exchange from a lesson shows:

T: A camel is not an insect. Why?
P: It hasn't got antennae.
T: A snail has got antennae.
P: Insects have wings.
T: So do nightingales.
P: Insects collect pollen.
T: So do humming birds.

Sequencing questions

Sequencing questions is a subtle art. A set of questions may each be sound, but together produce chaos. As indicated earlier, the linchpins of a sequence are often the responding moves of the teacher in between questions. The patterns that may emerge are shown below. In one of our research projects we found that, out of more than a thousand questions analysed, 53 per cent stood alone and 47 per cent were part of a sequence of two or more questions. Only 10 per cent of questions asked were in a sequence of more than four questions. Here is a variety of patterns observed in the lessons of teachers.

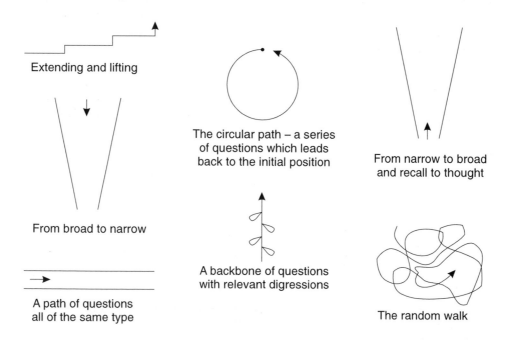

Extending and lifting

From broad to narrow

A path of questions all of the same type

The circular path – a series of questions which leads back to the initial position

A backbone of questions with relevant digressions

From narrow to broad and recall to thought

The random walk

Sequences of questions (based on Brown and Edmondson 1984)

Note: The random walk may be due to poor planning, personal disorganisation in the lesson or very distracting children

The notion of extending and lifting provided by Taba (1971) is particularly relevant here. Extending involves asking a series of questions at the same level before lifting the level of questions to the next higher level. Taba suggested that if pupils were to reach more complex levels of thought, they need ample opportunity to work at the lower levels by being asked for, or generating, their own examples and solutions.

Transcripts of lessons we have analysed, in which questions were thought to be used effectively, suggest that teachers have in mind key questions around which are clustered a large number of briefer, more direct and specific questions. The lessons develop a pattern which may not always take a straight line, but which is certainly not random.

Keeping a lesson on course is particularly difficult for newly qualified teachers. The temptation is to railroad the pupils in a way that is not appropriate, or to allow too much wandering away from the point of the lesson. A useful image here is *tacking*, as in sailing. You adjust your questioning so that you move from side to side through a lesson, yet stay on course. The image also reminds us that to stay on course you need to know what the course is, hence the importance of planning sequences based on key questions, and on preparing interesting material relevant to the questions being asked (see Unit 6).

Activity 8

1   Devise a sequence of four or five questions in your subject that could raise the level of thinking in a class. An example of a three-step sequence is:

Can you give me an example of something living?
What do plants need to help them grow?
How could we test out your idea that plants need water to grow?

2   Think back to a sequence of questions that you have used recently. Which pattern on the opposite page was it closest to? Using these patterns, try planning one of the sequences (not the random walk) and using it in a lesson. Consider how well you kept to the sequence.

Activity 9

1   Look at these two statements and decide what different effects they would produce in the classroom:

(a) 'Jill. What happens when these substances are heated together?'

(b) 'Now what happens when these substances are heated together? ... Jill?'

2   Read the following transcripts and identify examples of prompts, probes and other features of the tactics of questioning discussed in this unit.

Transcript 8

T: What do you remember about the legend of Robin Hood? Do you know anything about him?
P: He was in the woods.
T: That's right [pause] and what did he do?
P: Arm his bow and arrow.
T: Yes.

P: Trees and people.

T: What was he trying to do?

P: Trying to kill animals.

T: Was he? Wasn't he very nice then, Robin Hood?

P: No, not all the time, we watched a film about it. [Pause]

T: Who was his real enemy [pause] the Sheriff of … ?

P: The Sheriff of Not – Nott-ing-ham.

T: Do you remember who his friends were? Robin Hood had some really good friends. Who was that big fat man, Friar … ?

P: Friar erm erm.

P: Friar … Tuck.

T: Yes! You remember, and Little John who was his tall friend.

Transcript 9

T: What sort of a man was Scrooge? – Scott?

P: A stinge.

T: A stinge.

P: He didn't want to give his money away.

T: All right, he doesn't want to give any money away or anything – why?

P: Too grumpy.

T: He's a grumpy man, Mark, so he doesn't want anyone to feel happy, he doesn't want to give them anything. Good!

P: Selfish.

T: Carl thinks he's selfish and indeed the centre of his life is himself.

P: He is unhappy because when he was younger his girlfriend left him and he didn't want anyone too [i.e. didn't want another girlfriend].

T: That's absolutely true. Something sad happened to him and they never really got together and never married and he became miserable, he became selfish, he lived for himself – yes, April?

P: He's all stingy and tight and grumpy.

T: Stingy, tight and grumpy.

P: He doesn't care about anyone else.

T: Right, he doesn't care about anyone else – last one, John?

P: He like, um … er, never got enough money.

T: Right – never got enough money for what?

P: To um … he's the sort of person who could never give money away to any charity.

T: Does that mean he does not give money away to charity because he's so poor himself, John?

P: No, he's so rich and so mean.

T: That's right, he's rich and he is mean. We do know that he is a successful businessman and actually he has got quite a lot of money but he keeps that money for himself.

3   Audio-record part of one of your lessons in which you are asking questions. Take four or five minutes of that audio-recording which contain questions and produce a transcript of them. Analyse the tactics of questioning that you used. Pay particular attention to your pausing, pacing, prompting and probing.

4   Here are the ten most common tips that experienced teachers were found to have given beginners on the tactics of questioning. Which do you agree or disagree with, and why?

- Use a variety of both open and closed questions.
- Get the language right and choose words carefully.
- Listen carefully to children's answers.
- Be prepared to rephrase questions and redirect them.
- Keep questions brief and simple.
- Start from what the pupils know.
- Admit when you don't know yourself, but then find out the answers.
- Hands up and one at a time to answer.
- Give everyone a chance to answer at some time.
- Watch for diversions or 'silly' answers and discourage them.

Unit 4 What kinds of lessons do you teach?

There are as many different lessons as there are people teaching them, for even two lessons ostensibly on the same subject, using the same scheme, textbook, or equipment, will have become significantly different a few seconds after they have commenced, simply because of human diversity.

In some cultures, at various times, there have been attempts to standardise teaching. In ancient China, the Book of Rights, *Li Chi*, laid down in some detail how teaching should take place in such a way as to ensure no deviation from the norm: 'The teacher reads out the principles and the pupils repeat them after him, echoing every intonation and stress, and this is continued until the pupils are word perfect.' Wu Yun-duo, talking about this tradition of teaching in China, recalled his own experiences centuries later: 'The master never explained anything, and when I asked a question, he simply stared me into silence.' (Wragg, 1974).

The demands of the twenty-first century are substantial and if children were only to be submitted to a style of teaching that required them to sit and listen, or to copy exactly what the teacher did, they would be ill-equipped to face up to them. There are many types of lesson that teachers can plan, and the questions asked in class will often reflect the overall purpose and structure of the lesson itself, so before reading this unit you might like to tackle the following activity.

Activity 10

Spend a few minutes jotting down or thinking through in your mind the various kinds of lessons that you have taught. Compare your categories of lessons to those of a few colleagues. The term *lesson* is used here to include any structure for organising learning, such as practical or project work, as well as conventional classroom lessons. What kind of lessons do you prefer? Why? What did you think of first when tackling this activity?

Some teachers report that in attempting this activity they first thought of lessons in terms of *content* rather than *structure*. Indeed it is difficult, but often very revealing, to attempt to classify lessons in terms of structures. It can be salutary to discover that you are using the same basic structure for all your lessons, and only changing the content.

In this unit we describe four common types of lessons that can be found in schools. These types are labelled:

(1) exposition   (2) discussion   (3) skill   (4) investigative

Within each type there are variations and sometimes what begins as one type of lesson may deliberately or unintentionally be transformed or fused seamlessly into another type. What starts off as exposition can transmute into discussion, while an investigation can change to an exposition, especially if it has gone astray or moved too slowly. Within each major type, teachers often create their own mini-structures, so the four types we discuss are not exclusive.

EXPOSITION LESSONS

In exposition lessons the teacher explains, sometimes by asking questions, and pupils then answer. This type of lesson is often followed by individual learning tasks, although small group learning or investigations can follow it. The lesson may be a sequence of brief explanations and questions, or a chunk of presentation followed by lengthy questions and answers. The exposition may be based on all forms of content, from science to the exploration of legend. The pupils may be involved in various forms of learning: recitation, reasoning, imagining, speculating, evaluating.

Such lessons are known as *recitation lessons* in the United States. They are as old as teaching itself. They were used widely in the nineteenth century, in the early twentieth century and they are still in use today. There is no inherent weakness in such lessons if they engage pupils' interest and foster their learning, the weakness lies in using solely these kinds of lessons. Exposition lessons can form a valuable function if handled sensibly. The broad purposes of questioning in exposition lessons are:

1   To encourage pupils to talk, so they reveal what they already know and don't know.
2   To ensure that they have grasped the key points that link to earlier learning and which will link to subsequent learning.
3   To develop their understanding of what is being taught.

It follows that to make questions effective in exposition one needs to know one's topic and to estimate what the children may or may not know about it. A common error in exposition lessons, since the whole class is usually involved, is to ask only questions that everyone will be able to answer. Another is to ask questions simply to punctuate the teacher's monologue, not with a view to opening up a genuine dialogue. If pupils become frustrated by the controlled nature of the lesson they may seek to take it to points not intended, or the teacher may launch into an unintended and perhaps confusing explanation, in order to salvage the lesson.

Here are some pointers for improving the effectiveness of questions during exposition lessons. The suggestions are also relevant to other lessons. They are based upon proposals in Dillon (1988).

- Convert some of your exposition into a series of key questions.
- Before asking one of the key questions, prepare the way for it.
- Ask the questions nice and slowly, stop and think whether the question is right for the occasion. Ask and then stop your exposition for a while, so you can get the best out of pupils' answers.
- Listen to the answers, listen for the forthcoming answers, listen for all the answers, listen to right and wrong answers, and sustain the listening.

Questioning during an exposition lesson

The encouragement to 'stop and think' reminds us not to ask immediately the question that simply pops into our head, but to consider it briefly first to ensure that it is worthwhile. The question then has more chance of helping pupils to learn, rather than encouraging them to open their mouths. The injunction 'ask and stop' helps to avoid asking too many questions at once and gives time for pupils to think about a key question before they answer. A geography teacher, during what was predominantly an exposition lesson on the effects of motorways on adjoining communities, asked the key question, 'What will happen when the motorway reaches our town?' The resulting discussion helped focus the rest of what turned out to be a very interesting lesson to which pupils responded positively.

Listening to pupils' answers properly requires discipline. The answers that they give may not necessarily reveal what they know so much as what they think the teacher wants them to say. Their understanding may be imperfect even if their answer is correct. Alternatively, they may have answered a different question from the one that you thought you had asked. It is quite common for pupils to give socially acceptable responses to questions about personal, social and health education matters, such as condemning smoking, or respecting the environment, but then to behave quite differently away from the classroom.

DISCUSSION LESSONS

Discussion lessons may be characterised as conversations that go back and forth, over, through and round a topic. There is not a rigid structure so much as a flexible framework to the lesson. Expositions that become unintentional discussions usually lack even that framework. Discussions tend to have fewer questions, more spontaneous contributions from pupils and relatively more pupil-to-pupil exchanges, but there may still be few in absolute terms. In

'So, what have we learned about electricity today then?'

discussion lessons there is the problem of identifying the key questions to be discussed, since the more that pupils take responsibility for guiding and shaping the conversations, the less direct control the teacher has over content and direction. It may only be in retrospect, looking back over the lesson, that the key issues can be determined.

In discussion lessons teachers still need to think about the key questions on which they want to focus in the topic. For a fruitful discussion which allows pupils some significant say over what is discussed, while at the same time covering the ground that teachers judge to be important, it is best to think of questions that may be perplexing, intriguing or even puzzling to pupils. Skilfully chosen encouraging, broad questions are often effective in sparking off animated conversations. The process may begin with recall questions to extend and activate knowledge and then thought questions to lift the discussion. Some further suggestions on preparing discussion questions are given in Unit 6. As well as using broad questions you can also use alternative strategies, and some possibilities are given on the opposite page.

Using statements rather than questions is based on the notion that providing views and information can sometimes evoke more open responses than questions. Even in everyday conversation it is difficult to ignore certain challenging statements (Hey, I'm talking to you!). Making these kinds of statement in lessons, however, requires you to think about the questions that spring to mind and then to convert them into statements.

A common problem, during discussion lessons, especially when pupils are encouraged to take the lead, is getting lost. Put less bluntly, it is knowing how far to let a discussion move off its principal theme. The answer to this problem lies in (a) knowing how to chair a discussion effectively, and (b) not losing sight of the key questions for the topic. If you cannot see the connection, then either move the discussion back on course, or ask a pupil how what he is saying is related to the main question and the central topic.

1   Use a statement related to what the pupil has just said, and wait for a response.
2   Review your or other people's *experiences* with regard to the discussion.
3   Review your own or other people's *feelings* on the topic and ask a *Why?* question.
4   Indicate your acceptance of what a pupil has said and look to another pupil for a response.
5   Say nothing, but look interested and receptive, so that someone else is encouraged to talk.
6   Encourage pupils to ask questions of you and of each other.
7   Paraphrase/summarise the debate so far, or ask pupils to do this, then move on to next phase.

Alternatives to questions

SKILL LEARNING

Much of this book is about pupils acquiring knowledge, but skill learning is vital in our society when very high levels of skill are demanded – in some cases just for survival – so we shall spend a little more time on it in this section, for it is crucial to ask appropriate questions when teaching skills.

Alongside and based firmly upon the knowledge that pupils are expected to acquire, lies a whole series of skills. These can be manipulative dexterity, like handling specialist equipment and tools in a technology lesson, using a paintbrush, or psychomotor skills in sports activities, such as swimming, trampolining, gymnastics. Indeed, skills are often the prerequisites in learning new methods and theories. For example, keyboard skills are required in computing; manipulative skills are the basis of setting up and using intelligently scientific apparatus and survey instruments. When we enlarge the notion of skill to include cognitive skills, such as reading, writing, problem-solving, as well as social skills, like the ability to work harmoniously as a member of a team or become a good citizen, or if we consider the area of vocational education, then skills become not just a basis but a centrepiece.

All skills have components requiring us both to perceive and move in varying proportions. Copying from the blackboard is high on both perceiving and moving. Reading is higher on perceptual components. Skills usually are goal directed: they contain built-in feedback, which enables us to adjust our actions to the tasks in hand, and they are patterned sequences of actions in response to cues, rather than isolated instances of behaviour. Indeed, interactive technology can make instant feedback available in ways never previously thought possible.

In this section we focus upon the essentials of teaching someone else a skill and the use of questions and statements in such a task. Skill teaching may involve a whole class, a group of pupils or just one child. The basic principles, however, remain the same in these different circumstances. First, teachers need to reflect on or analyse the task; second, they or fellow pupils who already possess it may demonstrate the skill; third, they provide opportunities for practice with guidance; fourth, teachers monitor progress and provide feedback. Think of acquiring a relatively simple skill, like threading a needle. We analyse the task (the thread must go through the eye of the needle), someone might demonstrate for us (including handy tips like licking the end of the thread), we practise, under supervision, and then someone tells us, or we see for ourselves, how well or badly we are doing. Questions need to reflect these different phases and processes.

Task analysis

This is the key to successful preparation for teaching skills. One has to analyse what is involved in this skill and then design a sequence of tasks that are meaningful to the pupils. There are four types of task which are common.

1   Pupils are required to do something they already know, but in a different learning context (e.g. switching on a computer and opening a programme).
2   They have to learn an entirely new pattern of responses (catching or hitting a ball; learning to spell correctly).
3   They must sometimes learn how to complete a series of sub-tasks which are then joined together (hop, step and jump; handwriting).
4   They may have to combine new and old reactions in response to patterns of cues (copying a drawing; following a recipe).

> **Activity 11**
>
> Think of some examples of practical tasks that pupils tackle in your subject. Analyse and classify them, using steps 1 to 4 above. Note that what is new to a younger pupil may be commonplace to an older one.

Demonstration

Demonstrating consists of cueing appropriate actions by providing a model of a skill or set of skills, accompanied by statements and questions. The task is not easy. In order to give as near to a paragon model as possible, teachers often demonstrate themselves, or use a video showing some expert practitioner at work. This is fine, but there may be an unbridgeable gap between the adult expert's and the pupil's performance (or sometimes an embarrassingly small one if the teacher is not very good!). A concert pianist, for example, might completely overawe a beginner by giving the impression that the level of performance sought was way beyond the novice's potential. In supervising research in universities it is common to ask doctoral students to look at previous PhD theses in the library, so that they can see the finished model, but sometimes this kind of modelling has the opposite effect when newcomers say, 'I couldn't possibly do that'.

In order to avoid swamping newcomers under forbidding levels of competence, teachers sometimes ask pupils to demonstrate. The difficulty here is that pupil models may be too imperfect, the opposite extreme. In modern language teaching, for example, the more pupil modelling that takes place, the more learners may be bathed in each other's errors and gruesome mispronunciations. One reason why younger children in a family sometimes speak less well than did their eldest sibling at the same age is that the first child hears entirely adult models of speech, whereas later children hear the imperfections of their perhaps only slightly older brothers and sisters.

The big advantage of demonstration, however, is not only that it enables teachers to question pupils about what they notice or may need to do, but it also permits questions from pupils, 'Can you show us again?', 'Why do you have to do that first?', 'Will it still work if … ?', 'How do you … ?' For this reason it is often worth any risk involved.

In a technology lesson two pupils were not able to make the buggy that they had constructed run very far. It was powered by an elastic band that they had to twist round. The teacher asked them questions about the role of the elastic band and the forces involved and what would happen if they wound it up more times, or indeed too many times. He then got them to demonstrate the effects of two different degrees of winding. The positive result of this demonstration and the questions that accompanied it was a better understanding of the key scientific principles and their applications in technology.

Guidance

The pupil now tries to imitate the teacher's or other people's models while being provided with guidance. This may occur in the form of questions, like, 'Why didn't it work?' or, 'What do you need to do next?', or as statements, sometimes expressed in positive form, such as, 'Press lightly', sometimes in negative form, 'Don't press too hard.' Much questioning during guidance is in fact concerned with helping pupils to watch for the cues: 'Keep your eye on the ball' is a useful shorthand statement for such advice.

Feedback and questions

It is commonplace knowledge that precise relevant knowledge of results and positive feedback improve learning; unfortunately, it is not always common practice to give them. One reason for this is that, to be able to provide precise relevant knowledge of results, you must have conducted an analysis of the task so that you can point to the salient cues.

As well as providing knowledge of results and feedback you can also use questions to help pupils analyse their own performance. One of the strengths of interactive technology is that, if it has been skilfully constructed, it enables pupils to be given instant feedback about their errors, misconceptions, or their state of progress. Indeed, questioning has usually been built into the programs, both in the form of pupils having to answer questions as they proceed and also having the opportunity to interrogate the database on which they are working. The important matter of feedback is discussed more fully in the book *Explaining in the Secondary School* in this series.

INVESTIGATIVE LEARNING

Investigative learning involves experimentation or finding out by pupils them-selves. There are many forms of investigative learning and they vary in the time spent on the task, on the degree of openness of the task and the dependence on the teacher. Questioning strategies need to vary in accordance with the nature and complexity of the investigation, whether it is a simple routine experiment in science, for example, or an elaborate independent project by individuals and groups. Within the framework of investigative learning we can distinguish various levels of experiment, and the features that identify them are shown here.

	Level	Aim	Materials	Method	Answer
Demonstration	0	Given	Given	Given	Given
Exercise (Recipe)	1	Given	Given	Given	Given
Structured Enquiry	2	Given	Given	Part or Whole	Open or Part Given
Open Enquiry	3	Given	Open	Open	Open
Independent Project	4	Open	Open	Open	Open

Levels of experiment.

Small-scale projects with younger pupils are often at level 2. When operating at level 4 teachers can sometimes learn with and from their pupils, especially when they find themselves on unfamiliar ground in the subject, for example, when a physical scientist is supervising an independent investigation in genet-ics. The term 'independent' is used here, but 'semi-independent' would be a more honest description, because it is rare for pupils to be truly independent during investigations. If nothing else, they are legally under the supervision of their teachers, or following some agreed syllabus, albeit in a more exploratory way.

Investigative learning requires the use of a wide variety of thought ques-tions. Among these are speculative questions, evaluative questions and reason-ing questions. These questions often need to be planned and incorporated into the investigation. So, again, preparation is important (see Unit 6). All of this raises important questions about the role of the teacher in different circum-stances. During investigative lessons or learning sequences, the role of teacher moves closer to that of manager, adviser, guide, supporter and improver. These tasks are given in more detail on the opposite page.

The roles indicated may overlap, but they do provide a series of pointers for the way in which we might tackle investigative lessons. In addition to asking

Giving pupils the opportunity to take decisions

Director	Determining topic and method, providing ideas.
Facilitator	Providing access to resources and arranging programme of work.
Adviser	Helping to resolve problems and suggesting alternatives.
Instructor	Providing instruction when it is necessary.
Guide	Suggesting timetable for carrying out the investigation, writing up, giving feedback on progress and so on.
Critic	Commenting constructively upon the way the pupils are carrying out the investigation or interpreting the data.
Freedom giver	Giving pupils the opportunity to take decisions for themselves.
Supporter	Giving encouragement, showing interest, discussing pupils' ideas.
Manager	Checking progress regularly, monitoring what is going on, giving systematic feedback and helping the pupils to plan their work.
Examiner	Examining and appraising pupils' work and showing them at the end of the investigation how it could be improved even further.

Roles of the teacher in investigative lessons.

questions, however, teachers also have to carry out a number of activities that help pupils to learn on the spot. These are listed here.

- Anticipate and recognise the major difficulties that pupils experience.
- Ask questions that clarify understanding.
- Ask questions that clarify actions.
- Ask questions that guide the pupils to do the right things.
- Answer questions in a simple non-condescending way.
- Offer support and encouragement.

Some tasks for the teacher in investigative lessons.

Activity 12

1   Think of a particular skill, or set of skills, in a particular topic you might be teaching your class. Look at the roles described on the previous page, like director, instructor, critic, manager etc., and think of questions that might be asked when adopting that role.

2   Look at the two transcripts that follow, 11 and 12, and compare the two teachers' use of questions in their lessons in the light of some of the precepts discussed in the book so far. Which do you think is using questions more effectively and why?

Transcript 11

T: Let's just recap a little bit on what we have been doing. We started off with flight, didn't we, making what? Gliders first of all and we were using the air around us to make these things fly, weren't we? Can anyone remember what we learned about that? Right, if it had a pointed nose that was aerodynamic, that was the suggestion. What does 'aerodynamic' mean then? It's a very good word and a very important concept, what does it mean? The wind can pass through? Is that right? Cut through? Getting closer.

P: Cut over it.

T: Cut over it – yes! Do you actually mean that – the wind will cut through it or do you mean the dart itself will cut through the air? Right. So we found out that the shape was very important, wasn't it? Later on we will be finding out a little bit more about wind and how different shapes make a difference and we'll move on from there. From the paper darts we moved on to parachutes. What did you find out about air and parachutes – Nigel?

P: The air held up the parachute?

T: Right! What was pulling the parachute down?

P: Gravity.

T: Yes – weight, gravity was pulling it down. The weight, do you remember the parachute – what shape was it as it was falling? Do you remember somebody drew one pointed and we said that was wrong, didn't we? It was oval shaped.

P: Like a semi-circle.

T: A semi-circle, good. Why was it like that then, Sarah?

P: [inaudible from the tape]

T: Right! That's right. The air that was going into the parachute made the parachute expand at the top. Can you actually remember why we put a hole in the top of a parachute? Why did we put a hole in the top – Peter? Speak up so we can hear – why did we put a hole in the top?

P: To balance.

T: So it was balanced, good boy, well done! That's right, without it he couldn't keep his balance and he would move around. The hole in the top controls the air going out, doesn't it? Now we are moving on today, we are going to look at how we have used air, things that have moved through air and how we can use air, but today I want to introduce you to something else, the fact that air itself can move and we can use that air. What do we call, first of all, what do we call moving air outside? We've had a lot of it during the last few weeks, come on! It's obvious, Nicky.

P: Wind.

T: Wind. Right. Good. Moving air is called wind. Can wind affect our movements … can it affect movement? Pardon?

Transcript 12

T: Now. The first thing, we did this a little while ago, what we are going to think about this afternoon is why it is that birds can fly and we can't. Now what was one reason that we looked at after we looked at the TV programme? We had a go at doing something, what did we do, can anyone remember?

P: We made some flaps of our own and tried to get 3,000 in five minutes.

T: Three thousand flaps in a minute, wasn't it? Who was it that could do 3,000 flaps in one minute? Marina?

P: A bird.

T: Can you remember which bird?

P: A humming bird.

T: Right! It's a humming bird that could actually get 3,000 flaps in a minute. How close could we get to that?

P: I did 250.

P: 300.

T: 300. Well, I think some of our memories may be a little bit rusty, so we'll have another go. So stand up in a space so you're not too close to anyone and don't start until I tell you or you'll be worn out. I'll say, 'On your marks, get set, go.' [The pupils do the activity.] Now stop, right, sit down in your places again. Right. The first question I want to ask John is, how many birds have you seen that keep their wings still at the beginning and just flap the ends of them like you were doing?

P: He's always doing that!

T: Right. Sssh! How many did you manage, Marina?

P: 105.

T: Not bad. What about you, Alice?

P: 124.

T: Pretty good! Helena?

P: [No reply.]

T: David?

P: 206.

T: Pretty good! Adam?

P: 1,000.

T: 1,000! Are you sure? My goodness! You really must be aching, what about you?

P: 140.

T: That's pretty good, Lee.

P: 300.

P: He was counting in tens!

> *T:* John, with your sort of half-wings, how many did you do?
> *P:* 112.
> *T:* Stuart, what about you?
> *P:* 1,000.
> *T:* Are you sure? I think some of your counting methods have gone a bit astray there! Right. Did any of us manage 3,000?
> *P:* No.
> *P:* Nearly.
> *T:* Not quite. Why can't we manage 3,000?
> *P:* Our muscles aren't big enough.
> *T:* How big are your muscles, David? Where are your muscles?
> *P:* Here.
> *P:* Everywhere.
> *T:* What are muscles for?
> *P:* To make sure you can move.
> *T:* How do they work?
> *P:* If you didn't have any muscles you would just be flab and if you have got muscles then you can jump around and all that.
> *T:* Oh, very good! Thank you very much, John. We've got a picture here, let's see the picture for a minute and let's see if we can actually find a muscle and see what it's doing. Find this muscle here and rest your hand on top of it. [Puts hand on biceps]
> *P:* Mine go really high.
> *T:* How do you make it go really high then, John?
> *P:* You've got to flex it up and turn it round.
> *T:* That's right. Bring your arm up, can you feel it? Right. Let's give everyone a chance because you're all screaming at once, I can't hear what Alice and Marina are saying. Can you find yours, Alice?'
> *P:* Yes!

3   Read the following extract from a discussion lesson and comment on the teacher's ways of encouraging the pupils to talk. The lesson was about the relationships between ethnic groups. One pupil had observed that black police officers had a hard time.

Transcript 13

> *T:* That's a good point actually. It must be difficult [being a black police officer].
> *P:* The thing is if the black police officers try it with the white ones so that they actually think that they have to put up this sort of er, er, image and say, well, erm, I'm not really black.
> *T:* Like this?
> *P:* Yes.
> *T:* Yes?
> *P:* Yes, they should just be themselves really.
> *T:* But it's so easy to say, isn't it? You would have to be a very strong person to do that, wouldn't you?
> *P:* Yes, people won't talk to them and it's hard to work with people that won't talk to you and things like that.
> *T:* Yes.
> *P:* Because they've got to be two different people. They've got to be sort of someone at work and someone at home who's not a policeman.
> *T:* Yes.
> *P:* So erm, it must be really difficult.

P: Yeah, they've got to leave their work at work and just be themselves at home.

T: Yes.

4   Design and teach a brief investigative lesson. Identify the level of investigation that you are aiming at, using the categories on page 49. Design some discussion questions based on the investigation. At the end of the lesson, provide a brief summary (mini-exposition). If possible, teach the lesson you have planned, working with a colleague, so that you can observe and discuss the purposes, design questions and analyse the questions actually asked in the lessons. An added useful activity is to draw up a checklist of tactics that you would like your colleague to observe, for example, your use of pupils' ideas in developing the exposition summary.

5   Re-write some of the questions and explanations in the transcript above so that they would be more clear to the pupils. What do you change and why? Compare your suggested improvements with those of a few colleagues.

Unit 5 How do your pupils learn?

Ultimately the finest questions in the world would be useless if nobody learned anything of value, so this unit is about how children learn and how you can use questions to help them learn. It is not a treatise on different theories of learning or child development, as we simply focus on what you can do to help your classes learn whatever it is they are supposed to acquire as their own.

We also believe that *it is vital for pupils themselves to be brought in on the act of reflection*. If teachers can reflect on pupils' answers, why shouldn't children consider some of the same issues? In the book in this series on class management, the matter of self-discipline is raised. In the book on explaining, children are encouraged to explain to each other and to the teacher. The book on assessment and learning considers self-assessment. The topic of questioning, therefore, is

---

Activity 13

Step 1   Jot down your own thoughts on the following three questions:

1   How do the children in your class learn?
2   What prevents them from learning?
3   What sort of questions help them learn best?

Step 2   Give a class or a group of pupils a few minutes to write down answers to three parallel questions, phrased in the first person:

1   How do I learn?
2   Write down a question the teacher has asked you that you couldn't answer.
3   What sort of questions do I like? (Think of an example, don't just say 'easy ones'!)

Step 3   Discuss your thoughts with those of your pupils and any colleagues you have managed to dragoon into doing the same activity with one of their classes. What are the similarities and differences? What sort of questions do pupils like and dislike?

no different. It is a process that should be carried out *with* children, not just done *to* them. Some of the activities in this unit invite and provide structure for teachers to think about questions and answers with their classes, so we begin by considering these matters.

Teachers' personal theories of learning often arise out of practice and prior experience, rather than from reading. They can be circular and self-fulfilling, for the way we teach shapes the way that pupils respond and learn, which, in turn, may confirm our views of *how* they learn. For example, if we ask mostly questions that require simple recall, then most pupils will produce only short factual answers, often a single word, so we might conclude that children are only able to provide brief and self-evident responses. This may lead on to the erroneous view that children are not capable of profound thought, or that most of them are lazy intellectually.

APPROACHES TO TEACHING AND LEARNING

In Unit 4 we discussed the use of questions in some common types of lesson – exposition, discussion, skill learning and investigative learning. The question you need to ask yourself is, 'What is the most appropriate type of lesson and style of questioning for the task in hand and this particular group of children?' Given also the importance of evoking pupils' interest, arousing their curiosity, involving them in an active, rather than a passive way, a variety of approaches is most appropriate for helping them develop. We consider five key aspects below.

Active learning

Most children (and adults) learn best when actively involved. So it is useful to look critically at the range of activities that pupils do in your lessons and whether the overall pattern is too predictable. Within that broad pattern and the different phases of lessons, variety in questioning is also a valuable stimulus for active learning. It is also worthwhile setting up conditions for pupils to ask questions, so that they too become active inquisitors, not just the recipients of someone else's thinking about what needs to be learned. Morgan and Saxton (1994) describe how pupils can work in groups of two or three to work out questions for themselves. One group of 15-year-olds who were studying trees produced, among others, 'What chemical changes in leaves cause them to change colour?' and, 'How can I prevent the destruction of the rainforests of the world?'

Purpose learning

Activity *per se* is not enough. Children (and adults for that matter) often learn best when they can see what the purpose of an activity is and know what is expected of them. That is one reason why some young adults who have not done well at school may achieve better when they are in a job, attending vocational courses where they can see the immediate and longer-term purposes of learning. In some of the lessons that we observed in research projects, many pupils were active on the surface, but they were unsure underneath what they were supposed to be doing. The professed aims of these poorer lessons were laudable but often vague, as were their questions. By contrast, in more successful lessons teachers had realistic, concrete objectives about what the children would be learning and so their questions were more focused.

Safe learning

Children need to feel safe enough to take risks in their learning. Hence the importance of class management, of well-defined procedures and routines (see the volume in this series on *Class Management in the Secondary School*). Indeed, the absence of a safe and secure structure is the major obstacle to children, whether in the classroom, or in a laboratory, workshop, gym, swimming pool, or out on a field trip. No one learns well if they feel under threat. Managerial questions enable teachers to monitor safety, as well as assess and cope with risk.

Reflective learning

Reflective learning may at first sight seem possible only for mature learners, since they have deeper foundations on which to build. Yet reflection on learning should begin in primary school and continue right through secondary schooling and beyond, so that children learn to analyse, evaluate and explore their actions and thoughts. Much of reflective learning is based upon thought questions, so it is important for us to consider the thought questions we are going to ask our children if we wish to develop their reflective learning. Reflective learning involves learners questioning themselves: How am I doing? How did I do it? The first is related to self-assessment and the second to the processes of learning.

Responsible learning

Most of us learn best when we have a sense of responsibility and ownership for our own learning, a feeling that we are *party* to it, not the *victim* of it. Encouraging pupils, with support, to take some responsibility themselves, to organise and monitor their own learning, is a valuable long-term objective. There is a risk of confusing goals and means here, however, since it does not follow that, because responsibility is a long-term objective, we should make children solely responsible for their learning. Rather, it is important to teach them to be responsible learners through methods of teaching used, the learning tasks set, by encouragement and feedback. The use of questions is central to this endeavour, 'What do you think you need to do next?', 'Are you happy with what you've done so far?', 'What can you do if you're stuck, other than come and ask me?'

Activity 14

Teaching is often too busy to leave much time for scrutiny, but once in a while it is worth keeping a log for a day of the kinds of teaching that you do. You may use categories we have suggested, like exposition, discussion, skill and investigative learning, or your own categories plus additional categories showing when pupils are working on their own or in groups. For this purpose, divide your day into quarter-hour segments and record in a few words the major activity or activities during each segment. *Record from time to time a question you have asked during that time period.* Analyse the proportion of time devoted to each activity. Compare your profile with that of a few colleagues. Keeping a log is time-consuming, not to be recommended as a regular practice, because it takes away valuable teaching time. Once in a while, however, it can be a worthwhile analysis of a busy life and this can help planning.

9.00

9.15

9.30

9.45

10.00

10.15

10.30

10.45

11.00

11.15

11.30

11.45

12.00

12.15

12.30

12.45

1.00

1.15

1.30

1.45

2.00

2.15

2.30

2.45

3.00

3.15

3.30

3.45

4.00

4.15

4.30

4.45

On the opposite page is a list of pupil tasks often set or encouraged by teachers. Tick any that you used during the day that you logged and add them to the list. *Be on the lookout for any questions you ask during these different activities.* Again, compare your tasks and questions with those set or encouraged by your colleagues. Are your questions different (a) for each of the various activities, (b) from those asked by your colleagues? These activities are by no means comprehensive and some will invariably overlap more than one category, so it should also be illuminating to list other activities in your teaching which are not down on this list.

1   Completing work sheets.
2   Working with programmed or computer-based material.
3   Copying notes from a board or other source.
4   Writing workbook exercises.
5   Solving problems.
6   Summarising thoughts in a plan.
7   Small group discussions/activities.
8   Whole class interactive teaching.
9   Whole class, little interaction, teacher solo.
10 Working in pairs.
11 Guided reading in response to a question.
12 Completing multiple-choice true/false tests.
13 Writing a brief report.
14 Preparing material for a class magazine.
15 Carrying out an enquiry or experiment.
16 Writing up the results of the enquiry/experiment.
17 Demonstrating to other pupils.
18 Writing stories.
19 Preparing questions on what is being studied.
20 Preparing display materials for use around the classroom.
21 Looking for facts in a book, a database or the internet.
22 Analysing data collected in the field or in the classroom.
23 Preparing charts or models.
24 Illustrating or representing ideas pictorially.
25 Map making or completing.
26 Short practice drills.
27 Making estimations before calculating them more exactly.
28 Creating graphs, pictures or models.
29 Seeking or discussing applications of principles to everyday life.
30 Measuring.
31 Reporting on events.
32 Organising facts and principles gathered from discussion.

Some pupil activities

All this is fine in an ideal world, but the mirror image of the question about how pupils learn is, 'Why do pupils sometimes *not* learn?' Moreover, could some kind of engagement with them, involving questioning, help to improve learning? Activity 15 is taken from a lesson where there was little attention being paid by pupils to the task in hand and the teacher's failure to involve pupils in the proposed activity contributed to the inattention. See if you can find ways of restructuring what went on.

1   This transcript was taken from a lesson in which many of the class were not conce ntrating and the teacher was often distracted. Read the transcript to establish what the teacher was trying to do (get the class to write a piece about a badger). How would you have tackled the task? The teacher talks without engaging pupils (indeed, she usually stops those who seek to join in and often repeats herself), and the questions asked tend to be rhetorical, neither expecting nor securing a response. *Decide where and what sort of questions the teacher might have asked, with a view to engaging pupils' interest more,* turning an interrupted monologue into a fruitful dialogue.

Transcript 14 The Badger

P: Miss, there's a certain way to stroke a badger.

T: Before we go any further you need your reading book, so if you haven't got it in a moment, don't go yet … reading book you need … you need the two pieces of paper I have given you, a pen or pencil, whichever you feel comfortable writing with, a ruler for your margins. You can share a ruler if somebody's got it on the table and you've forgotten one, put them on now, both sides and write your name on the top. What do you need, a pencil? Here we go, do it on both sides and then you'll be ready. It doesn't matter if you don't write on both sides, you've got it if you need it. Piece of paper for you, close this book up a minute, right there you are, close this up. Put your name on the top, no, OK, that's the business side of getting ready. You've got your paper ready and your name is on the top. If you haven't put your name on the top it doesn't matter which side you put the name on the top now. They're in the way, Tim, put them down on the floor, down there, don't worry about it, all you need is your name. No, don't worry about using to write with because then I want you to listen to me. Right! Now I know you are all listening when you are looking at me. Right. Just a few people I'm waiting for. Right, Tim, Kevin, are you ready? If you look at me then I know that you are ready. Good boy! Turn round a little bit. Now yesterday in the afternoon we did an awful lot of talking, I did a lot of talking and we looked at a video and we looked at our badger. Now today for our piece of writing you are going to be thinking about the badger. You're going to be thinking about the badger in lots and lots of ways. You can decide what kind of way you would like to write your piece of writing; it could be that you're going to write me a story, it could be that you're the kind of person who likes to write facts. Now your piece of writing is going to be your choice, but I'm going to put lots of ideas to you and you could put some ideas back to me in a minute. Hands down until I'm ready. But your piece of writing is going to be your choice, but I'm going to put lots of ideas to you and you could put some ideas back to me in a minute. Hands down until I'm ready. But your piece of writing today, remember what we spoke about yesterday, is going to be your best piece of writing because it's going to go in your file. All right? So you're going to do your neatest writing, not worrying too much about spelling but thinking about it and thinking, 'Yes, I think I know that word.' All right, but don't worry if you can't spell it, put the nearest spelling that you know. Wait a minute – think about doing the best piece of work that you've done for a long time. All right? Now let's think about what we could write about badgers. No! Remember from yesterday how I said don't call out. Put your hand up if you've got an idea. That would be a very good piece to do because you could do the badger's fears and the kind of environment he was in, where he was running to or where he was hiding. Lots of description could come into that.

2   *Answers to questions* are also a matter that should be shared with pupils. The following activity may be used to get them to consider what counts as 'good' answers.

(i)   Set a simple exercise on a topic requiring pupils to give their views on some aspect of a subject, like writing five to ten lines on, 'How do people pollute the environment and what could be done to prevent or reduce pollution?'

(ii) Before the pupils reveal their answers, discuss with them what they think are the features of 'good' and 'weak' answers to the question and put three or four answers of differing quality on the board. For example, a 'weak' answer might be inaccurate, unsupported by evidence, or based on hearsay and superstition, rather than scientific fact. Ask the pupils to read the answers and to try to decide which is best and why. Develop a discussion on this theme. You will probably have to use all the skills that were described earlier in this text. Summarise the main points of what constitutes good answers to your question.

(iii) Examine the differences between spoken answers, such as are given during class discussion, and written answers.

(iv) Mark their written answers carefully, praising the good points and suggesting ways of improving upon their answers, in the light of the discussion. You may find the following checklist helpful to you and your pupils, though you may have to modify it, depending on the subject matter.

Checklist

- Is my answer clear? Am I using understandable English in the answers and not confusing the person who is listening to me, or reading my answer?
- Is my answer accurate? Have I given facts and figures that are not true?
- Is my answer appropriate? Have I answered the question that was asked?
- Is my answer specific? Will the teacher or the person reading my answer know who and what I am writing about?
- Does my answer contain support for my views? Have I given reasons, facts or examples to support my opinions or argument?
- Does my answer show an awareness of complexity? Have I looked at more than one side of the question?

Responsible learning

Unit 6 Are you 'prepared' to ask questions?

Seconds into any lesson it will have taken an unpredictable turn. Even if you are teaching familiar subject matter with a class you know well, you cannot predict *exactly* what will happen beyond some rough guesses. In this unit we explore the preparation of questions and, because one cannot prepare questions without considering the context and purposes of the lesson in which the questions occur, we also consider lesson preparation.

PREPARING QUESTIONS

As a preliminary to preparing questions, it is useful to consider these two questions:

1   What *can* I ask the class?
2   What *should* I ask the class?

A useful approach to 'What can I ask the class?' is to brainstorm the questions. Think of a topic you are likely to teach and then take a blank sheet of paper and write down on it as many questions as you can within five minutes – do not worry about the appropriateness or quality of the questions at this stage. Once you have done this, you can begin to sift the questions and arrive at those you will ask the pupils. Inevitably, this leads you to consider what your objectives are and what the class might already know.

Using key questions

Many teachers use a number of *key questions* to structure and provide links in their lessons. For example, in a lesson we observed on 'prejudice' three of the key questions were, 'What do you understand by the word *prejudice*?', 'Which individuals or groups are likely to experience prejudice?' and, 'How does prejudice show itself in everyday life?' It produced a lively discussion about numerous issues: different age groups like teenagers and the elderly, ethnic and religious minorities, conformity and non-conformity, emotional bias and the nature of evidence. It was excellent 'citizenship' material in what was ostensibly an English lesson.

Sometimes teachers we have observed did not seem to use key questions well. A few appeared to think that 'key' questions were any questions they asked. On many occasions the first key question asked by teachers was a 'What … ?' question, although 'How?', 'Why?', 'Do you think … ?', 'Which … ?' were also used. It would be tempting to say that 'What?' questions got poor answers and 'How?' questions were thought provoking. In fact, 'What' questions produced both poor (i.e. unanswerable, dull, pointless) and good (stimulating, enjoyable, multi-faceted) responses. 'How?' questions could also be either thought pro-voking or pointless. It was the *content* of the question and its appropriateness to the audience and the subject matter, not its form, that usually determined success.

The same can be said of the succeeding key questions in a lesson, after the opener. Below are a few pointers from our analysis of transcripts which may be of interest when you are considering your own use of key questions.

Timing

Here are some key questions we observed, with comments on their timing.

> *'What is friction?'* was asked too early by the teacher in a prrimary science lesson. It was asked before the investigation when it would have been better asked and discussed after the children had some experience of the experiments they were to conduct on friction.

> *'What is a neighbourhood watch scheme?'* The children had already done some work on this before the question was asked, and they could tell the teacher some relevant stories about neighbourhood watch schemes.

> *'How do you think it felt?'* The children had experienced a sense of drama and impending threat to a particular character in a story. The invitation to empathise produced some imaginative answers that seemed to stimulate others to provide inventive answers also.

Key questions need not be asked at the beginning of a lesson. Indeed, they can be used to summarise what the children have just learned, so be wary of asking your key questions too early. Never be afraid of asking thought-provoking questions at the right time, nor of spontaneously thinking up a key question during a lesson in the light of its development.

Level

Earlier, we mentioned some points about levels of questioning and the proper language register and thought processes appropriate to different circumstances. Here are further questions we have witnessed, with comments on their level.

'*What is the colour of the snow?*' This question was so ridiculously easy for the 12-year-olds of whom it was asked in a geography lesson that no one replied, thinking that there must be a catch. Some teachers we observed asked only questions that everybody in the class could answer. Repeating these questions, as a few teachers tried, does not work at all well.

'*How could you design a home for these owls?*' This question was too difficult for the class, because they had too little information either about owls or bird habitats. The children floundered and couldn't sort out what was required of them. The question needed supporting by relevant information first, or breaking down into separate components.

'*What is the difference between a wing and an arm?*' This looked like a mind-boggling question, but in fact it worked well because the class were able to identify several differences and the teacher then was able to help the children classify them.

The best key questions often contained a sense of looking ahead, of helping the lesson to move on. The least effective questions seemed to be going nowhere, or only back to what the pupils already knew. Some suggestions for the use of key questions are encapsulated in the mnemonic IDEA.

I   Identify the key questions in relation to your objectives for the lesson.
D   Decide on the level and order (timing) of the questions.
E   Extend the questioning. Think of supplementary and subsidiary questions to ask.
A   Analyse the answers that you are likely to receive and the responses that you might give.

IDEA on questions.

PREPARING LESSONS

Many textbooks on teaching advocate the setting of objectives, choice of methods of teaching, pupil tasks and assessment. What these texts do not tell you is that few teachers actually plan their lessons in this order, although the product may be expressed in this form. The thinking processes involved in lesson preparation are less tidy and often more creative than a direct application of teaching by behavioural objectives (see Clarke and Petersen, 1986).

The preparation of lessons may be construed in the form of three simple questions:

1   What do I want my pupils to learn?
2   How do I want them to learn it?
3   How will I find out whether they have learned it?

Using a mind map

Most teachers approach these questions through considering not only *content*, but also *experience, activities* and *methods*. A mind map is a helpful way into these questions (see the diagram). To construct a mind map you write down the topic of a lesson in the centre of a page and then write down a set of sub-topics or questions around the topic. This may lead to further division of the sub-topics or to another sub-topic.

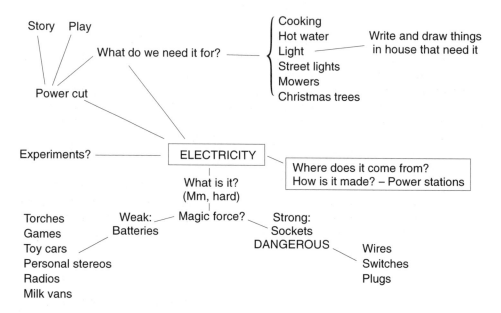

The beginnings of a mind map

The next step is to redraw or tidy up the mind map, so that similar topics are clustered together. At this stage you can begin to identify the key questions that might structure the lesson. Note that these particular key questions are not necessarily the questions that you might ask the pupils. Some of them may be the questions that underlie the questions that you are going to ask.

A mind map provides the basis for thinking about any kind of topic or lesson. It may also be used during a lesson to move discussion on, to keep on track and to summarise. Once the mind map is completed, the next step is the choice of pupil task and the method of teaching. This brings us to the question, 'How am I going to get pupils to learn it?'

To answer this question, you may have to rummage through materials, ideas in your own head, or even invent quite new learning materials. Then comes the choice of method of teaching – although often you move between thinking about pupils' learning methods and the teaching methods. Last, but not least, you have to build into the tasks the opportunities to find out what the pupils have learnt. These include the use of oral questions, assessing project group and individual work.

The GAITO approach

An alternative or supplementary approach to the use of a mind map is the GAITO approach:

Goals, Activities, Input, Timing, Order.

In this approach you consider what you want the pupils to learn, as well as their goals and the activities that you want them to undertake. You then consider what specific contributions you will make through exposition and questions. Estimate the time required for each segment – and allow for slippage. Consider then the order of the lesson. Incidentally, often the last thing you think of is the first thing that you should do in a lesson. Also consider various pathways through the materials, for your pupils may not respond quite as you expect. You cannot predict accurately how a particular lesson will develop, but you can be prepared for most developments.

Finally, it is worth pointing out that most teachers find preparing topics or themes easier than preparing specific lessons, for a topic or theme is a meaningful chunk in one's own head, but the individual lessons may not be so clear. Hence, there is much to be said in favour of preparing sets of lessons on a topic using mind maps, GAITO and key questions.

Activity 16	
1	Prepare a lesson on a topic of your choice. Include three or four pre-planned *key questions*. How do you think pupils will respond to them? If possible ask a colleague to do the same exercise, but work independently at this stage.
2	Make an audio- or video-recording of the lesson. Before listening to the recording, identify what you think were the key questions in it. Listen for them and the pupils' answers. How accurate were you in your predictions? How could your use of key questions in that lesson have been improved?
3	Brainstorm ways in which you and your colleague might improve your questions. Reciprocal working of this kind can be very helpful for two teachers wanting to help each other to improve professional skills.
4	*If you still have the recording from the first lesson you recorded in this book in Activity 2, listen to it again* and consider in what ways you have improved your approach to questioning. How might you now improve your questioning even further?

References

Ausubel, D.P. (1978) *Educational Psychology: A Cognitive View*, New York: Holt, Rinehart and Winston.

Barnes, D. (1969) 'Language in the secondary classroom', in Barnes, D., Britton, J. and Rosen, H. (eds) Language, the Learner and School, Harmondsworth: Penguin.

Barnes, D. and Todd, E. (1977) *Communication and Learning in Small Groups*, London: Routledge and Kegan Paul.

Brown, G.A. (1978) *Microteaching: A Programme of Teaching Skills*, London: Methuen.

Brown, G.A. and Edmondson, R. (1989) 'Asking questions', in Wragg, E.C. (ed.) *Classroom Teaching Skills*, London: Routledge.

Clarke, C.M. and Petersen, P.L. (1986) 'Teachers' thought processes', in Wittrock, M. (ed.) *Handbook of Research on Teaching* (third edition), New York: Macmillan.

Dillon, J.T. (1981) 'To question or not question in discussion', *Journal of Teacher Education*, 32, 51–5.

—— (1988) *Questioning and Teaching: A Manual of Practice*, London: Croom Helm.

—— (1994) *Using Discussions in Classrooms*, Buckingham: Open University Press.

Edwards, A.D. and Furlong, V.J. (1978) *The Language of Teaching*, London: Heinemann.

French, P. and Maclure, M. (1983) 'Teachers' questions and pupil answers: an investigation of questions and answers in the infant classroom', in Stubbs, M. and Hillier. H., *Readings in Language, Schools and Classrooms*, second edition, London: Methuen.

Gall, M.D. (1970) 'The use of questioning in teaching', *Review of Educational Research*, 40, 707–21.

Gall, M.D. and Artero-Boneme, M.T. (1994) 'Questioning' in Husen, T. and Postlethwaite, T.N. (eds) *International Encyclopaedia of Educational research (second edition)* 8: 4875–82, Oxford: Pergamon.

Galton, M., Simon, B. and Croll, P. (1980) *Inside the Primary Classroom*, London: Routledge and Kegan Paul.

Haynes, H.C. (1935) 'The relationship of teacher instruction, teacher exposition and type of school to types of question.' Unpublished doctoral dissertation. Baltimore, MD: Peabody College for Teachers.

Kerry, T. (1989) 'Analysing the cognitive demands made by classroom tasks in mixed-ability classes', in Wragg, E.C. (ed.) *Classroom Teaching Skills*, London: Routledge.

Morgan, N. and Saxton, J. (1994) *Asking Better Questions*, Markham, Ontario: Pembroke Publishers.

Pate, R.T. and Bremer, N.H. (1967) 'Guiding learning through skilful questioning', *The Elementary School Journal*, 67, 417–22.

Piaget, J. and Inhelder, B. (1969) *The Psychology of the Child*, London: Routledge and Kegan Paul.

Rowe, M.B. (1978) *Teaching Science as Continuous Enquiry*, New York: McGraw-Hill.

Stevens, R. (1912) *The Question as a Measure of Efficiency in Instruction*, Teachers College Contribution to Education No.48, New York: Teachers College Press.

Taba, H. (1971) *Teaching Strategies and Cognitive Function in Elementary School Children*, San Francisco: San Francisco State College.

Tobin, K. (1987) 'The role of wait time in higher cognitive learning', *Review of Educational Research*, 57, 69–95.

Turney, C. *et al.* (1973) *Sydney Microskills*, Sydney: University of Sydney.

Wragg, E.C. (1974) *Teaching Teaching*, Newton Abbot: David and Charles.

—— (1989) *Classroom Teaching Skills*, London: Routledge.

—— (1993) *Primary Teaching Skills*, London: Routledge.

Learning to Teach Subjects in the Secondary School Series

Edited by Susan Capel, Marilyn Leask and Tony Turner

Designed for all students learning to teach in the secondary school and particularly those on school-based initial teacher training courses, the books in this series complement our best-selling textbook *Learning to Teach in the Secondary School* and its companion *Starting to Teach in the Secondary School*.

Learning to Teach in the Secondary School
A Companion to School Experience   2nd Edition
Susan Capel, Marilyn Leask and Tony Turner

1999: 504pp
Pb: 0–415–19937–9: £16.99

The series also includes:

Learning to Teach Geography in the Secondary School
A Companion to School Experience
David Lambert and David Balderstone

2000: 516pp
Pb: 0–415–15676–9: £18.99

Learning to Teach Science in the Secondary School
A Companion to School Experience
Tony Turner and Wendy DiMarco

1998: 352pp
Pb: 0–415–15302–6: £16.50

Learning to Teach Design and Technology in the Secondary School
A Companion to School Experience
Gwyneth Owen-Jackson

2000: 184pp
Pb: 0–415–21693–1: £16.99

Learning to Teach RE in the Secondary School
A Companion to School Experience
Edited by Andrew Wright and Anne-Marie Brandom

2000: 336pp
Pb: 0–415–19436–9: £16.50

Learning to Teach Art and Design in the Secondary School
A Companion to School Experience
Edited by Nicholas Addison and Lesley Burgess

2000: 392pp
Pb: 0–415–16881–3: £16.99

Learning to Teach English in the Secondary School
A Companion to School Experience
Jon Davison and Jane Dowson

1997: 352pp
Pb: 0–415–15677–7: £16.50

Learning to Teach History in the Secondary School
A Companion to School Experience
Terry Hadyn, James Arthur and Martin Hunt

1997: 320pp
Pb: 0–415–15453–7: £16.50

Learning to Teach Mathematics in the Secondary School
A Companion to School Experience
Edited by Sue Johnston-Wilde, Peter Johnston-Wilde, David Pimm and John Westwell

1999: 288pp
Pb: 0–415–16280–7: £16.50

Learning to Teach ICT in the Secondary School

A Companion to School Experience

Edited by Marilyn Leask and Norbert Pachler

1999: 296pp
Pb: 0–415–19432–6: £16.50

Learning to Teach Modern Foreign Languages in the Secondary School

A Companion to School Experience

Norbert Pachler and Kit Field

1997: 416pp
Pb: 0–415–16281–5: £16.50

Learning to Teach Physical Education in the Secondary School

A Companion to School Experience

Susan Capel

1997: 368pp
Pb: 0–415–15301–8: £16.50

Starting to Teach in the Secondary School

A Companion for the Newly Qualified Teacher

Susan Capel, Marilyn Leask and Tony Turner

1996: 320pp
Pb: 0–415–13278–9: £16.50

All these books are available from your normal bookshop or supplier. If you require further information, or the RoutledgeFalmer catalogue, please call Huw Neill on +44 0207 842 2152, or look at our website on www.routledgefalmer.com

Photocopiable Practical Resources for Secondary Schools

NEW
Stress Management Programme for Secondary School Students

Sarah McNamara

This is a resource pack for teachers to use in classrooms to help students combat stress. More and more young people suffer from stress nowadays, some of it school-related, some of it generated from home or friends. There are many causes, be it revision or exam pressure, bullying, low self-esteem, family problems, relationship problems, eating disorders or something else. Teachers are often the first people to notice this stress manifest itself and are more than likely the people who will have to deal with it.

As well as theory, this book has photocopiable worksheets included with it. The information is presented in an accessible way and there are plenty of follow-up activities and strategies for coping. Everything is geared towards making it readable and interesting for young people and teachers, but it never loses sight of the curriculum.

January 2001: A4: 112pp
Pb: 0–415–23839–0: £29.99

Using Data for Monitoring and Target Setting
A Practical Guide for Teachers

Ray Sumner and Ian McCallum

Are you keeping track of standards in your school?

A clear and practical guide to teachers and school administration staff that shows how to use spreadsheets and create orderly records of assessment. These can be used for the sort of statistical analyses that are now being demanded from schools. This photocopiable guide includes practical examples, step-by-step instructions, simple advice on how to use EXCEL and pictures of the actual screens you will be using.

1999: 100pp
Pb: 0–415–19686–8: £27.50

All these books are available from your normal bookshop or supplier. If you require further information, or the RoutledgeFalmer catalogue, please call Huw Neill on +44 0207 842 2152, or look at our website on www.routledgefalmer.com

Classroom Behaviour Management Titles from RoutledgeFalmer

NEW
Educating Children with AD/HD
A Teacher's Manual

Paul Cooper and Fintan O'Regan

Attention Deficit/Hyperactivity Disorder (AD/HD) is the most common behavioural disorder affecting up to 5% of children in the UK. This book provides a concise and comprehensive guide to educating children with AD/HD. It offers a theoretical introduction to AD/HD and practical guidance to the classroom teacher on how to support children with this condition.

The book is rooted in the experience of practitioners who work on a daily basis with children with AD/HD, and draws upon up-to-date research evidence on the topic. The authors challenge crude assumptions about AD/HD and argue that the best way to understand AD/HD is as a condition in which biological and environmental factors interact. Suitable for use as a teaching manual and a training resource, *Educating Children with AD/HD* will help teachers, other educational workers and students develop a sense of empowerment in relation to AD/HD to teachers.

June 2001: 112pp
Pb: 0–415 21387–8: £25.00

Surviving and Succeeding in Difficult Classrooms

Paul Blum

Focusing on the secondary school, but of great value to classroom teachers everywhere, this book offers sensible, practical advice on what to do to survive and succeed in the face of troublesome classroom behaviour.

'This is an excellent book in that it provides guidance to new teachers on the foundation of good classroom behaviour management and it is also recommended reading for staff tutors wishing to provide mentoring support for colleagues.' – *School Leadership and Management*

'This is a book for teachers ... nobody before has managed to convey the extent and degree of ill-discipline with such clarity.' – Peter Kingston of the *Guardian*

1998: 160pp
Pb: 0–415–18523–8: £12.99

All these books are available from your normal bookshop or supplier. If you require further information, or the RoutledgeFalmer catalogue, please call Huw Neill on +44 0207 842 2152, or look at our website on www.routledgefalmer.com

Inclusive Education Books
from RoutledgeFalmer

Special Educational Needs in Schools
2nd Edition

Sally Beveridge

This new edition of Sally Beveridge's renowned work provides a concise but comprehensive overview of key issues in provision for children with special needs in schools, emphasising the role of the mainstream classroom teacher. This second edition looks at the numerous changes in special educational policy and practice that have taken place in the past five years. Topics covered include:

- Concepts of SEN
- The legislative framework
- The range of special educational need and provision
- Teaching approaches and organisational strategies
- Frameworks of support

1999: 160pp
Hb: 0–415–20293–0: £42.50
Pb: 0–415–20294–9: £13.99

Photocopiable Resource
The Special Educational Needs Co-ordinator's Handbook
A Guide for Implementing the Code of Practice

Garry Hornby, Gregan Davies and Geoff Taylor

'It offers clear guidelines through the assessment procedures and supplements them with helpful proformas and illustrative material ... all in all, it should enhance the educational provision offered to pupils with special needs by helping schools to implement the Code of Practice effectively.' – *Times Educational Supplement*

'Easy to read and well-organised. The *Handbook* will be a useful resource in responding to the Code and in stimulating solutions to the challenges.' – *Educational Research*

'This publication will provide concrete support in making action for SEN pupils a reality in your school.' – *Junior Education*

1995: A4: 192pp
Pb: 0–415–11683–X: £27.50

All these books are available from your normal bookshop or supplier. If you require further information, or the RoutledgeFalmer catalogue, please call Huw Neill on +44 0207 842 2152, or look at our website on www.routledgefalmer.com